MW00903097

Jane Vogel

Grill It or Skillet

Jane Vogel

Jane Vogel

Grill It or Skillet

outskirtspress
DENVER, COLORADO

The opinions expressed in this manuscript are solely the opinions of the author and do not represent the opinions or thoughts of the publisher. The author has represented and warranted full ownership and/or legal right to publish all the materials in this book.

Grill It or Skillet
All Rights Reserved.
Copyright © 2012 Jane Vogel
v3.0 r1.2

Cover Photo © 2012 photos.com. All rights reserved - used with permission.

This book may not be reproduced, transmitted, or stored in whole or in part by any means, including graphic, electronic, or mechanical without the express written consent of the publisher except in the case of brief quotations embodied in critical articles and reviews.

Outskirts Press, Inc.
http://www.outskirtspress.com

ISBN: 978-1-4327-9387-6

Outskirts Press and the "OP" logo are trademarks belonging to Outskirts Press, Inc.

PRINTED IN THE UNITED STATES OF AMERICA

Welcome to the "Grill It or Skillet" World!

SIMPLE INGREDIENTS + SIMPLE PREP = SIMPLY DELICIOUS!!

Featuring only easy-to-prepare, tasty, and healthy meals and snacks, "Grill It or Skillet" brings you simple recipes using simple ingredients and simple tools.

- ***No special ingredients*** No arugula, no orzo, no "what the heck is that?" stuff!
- ***No special tools*** No need to buy a fancy new "whatever" -- actually nothing requiring electricity is used for any recipe in the book!

These recipes can be prepared almost anywhere—on a tailgate or picnic table at a park, a beach, a weekend swim meet or soft pitch tournament, on a boat, at a campground, at the cabin--you really don't even need a kitchen! (But if you have one, that's great, too.) Everything that needs to be cooked can be done on a portable propane or charcoal grill, over an open wood fire, or on a stove. Tools? Pans? Nothing more than just a skillet, small pan, and some aluminum foil.

You'll notice that many ingredients are used repeatedly throughout the book. If you don't have a certain spice, perhaps ground ginger, for example, if you do have to go buy it to make a selected recipe, you can be certain that ingredient will be called for in other recipes in this book. You won't just use it once and then never again. Keeping it simple!

To make it easier for you, the cook, consider making up a basic "kitchen bin" to carry with you. (If you're going to be in raccoon territory, get a bin that requires thumbs to open!) Include paper plates----please don't use foam, they just add to the landfill problem--- utensils, potholders, basic spices, baggies for leftovers, skewers, and so on. See the suggested list on the following page. Then simply restock the bin after you get home so it's ready for your next outing. – Also take a look at "Cooler Basics" for some helpful hints.

KITCHEN BIN BASICS

- a clear, "see through" bin with a latching type lid, about 22 x 16 x 14 tall
- a shoe-box size plastic box with a lid to keep basic spices: salt, pepper, garlic salt, ground ginger, dill weed, dried chives, lemon pepper, seasoned salt
- fire starter: long nosed "clicker" highly recommended, wooden matches
- paper plates: various sizes
- flatware: ample forks and spoons, fewer knives
- paper toweling
- can opener/bottle opener
- hamburger turner/metal spatula
- non-metal spatula if your pans are non-stick
- long handled tongs for the grill
- 2 large serving spoons, one slotted
- sharp knives: chef's knife, paring knife, steak knife (1 per diner or share!)
- dishwashing liquid detergent---keep in a sealed plastic bag to catch any drips
- dish cloth, dish towels, scratchy pad/scouring pad for pans
- hand towels (2-3)
- spring type clothespins
- potholders (2)
- pans: large skillet, small skillet, 8 qt. pan, 3 quart pan, and 1 quart pan—all with covers

COOLER BASICS

- Cooling sources: Ice cubes in bags, not loose (to contain melting water and prevent "swimming" cooler contents); ice frozen in a plastic 9 x 13 cake pan and kept at the bottom of a large cooler; frozen commercial chilling blocks or containers; frozen food which will be consumed during the outing; frozen juice concentrate, juice boxes or pouches
- Keep separate coolers for beverages and for food and instruct everyone to *stay out of the food cooler!* NOTE: Loose ice is great in the beverage cooler, just not in the food cooler.

Contents

APPETIZERS
SNACKS
HORS D'OUEVRES

SPREADS

SALMON AND HORSERADISH SPREAD

1—15.5 ounce can pink salmon

1—8 ounce cream cheese or Neufchatel (1/3 less fat)

¼ cup sour cream or lite sour cream

¼ cup prepared horseradish (not horseradish sauce)

1 tablespoon pickle relish—dill or sweet, either one

¼ teaspoon salt

¼ teaspoon garlic powder

- Soften cream cheese to make it easier to combine with other ingredients.
- Drain the salmon, remove the larger bones (small ones can stay), and flake with a fork.
- Combine all ingredients and thoroughly mash.
- Chill and serve on crackers or flatbread.

CHEDDAR CHEESE AND PECAN BALL *This is a very old recipe, compliments of my mother.*

1—8 ounce package shredded Cheddar cheese (Don't use "no fat".)

1--4 ounce package cream cheese or Neufchatel (1/3 less fat)

1 cup chopped pecans or pecan pieces, separated into half-cups

1 ounce diced pimentos (optional, but nice color)

¼ teaspoon garlic salt

¼ teaspoon onion salt or seasoned salt

- Soften cream cheese to make it easier to combine with other ingredients.
- Combine all ingredients thoroughly.
- Shape into a ball and roll in pecan pieces.
- Chill and serve with crackers.

GREEN ONION CHEESE SPREAD

1--8 oz. package cream cheese or Neufchatel (1/3 less fat)

2-3 tablespoons milk

½ cup sliced green onions

- Soften cream cheese to make it easier to combine with other ingredients.
- Thoroughly combine milk and cream cheese.
- Stir in green onions and chill.
- Serve with crackers or pretzels or hard, pencil-like bread sticks.

ANOTHER IDEA: Add ½- ¾ cup picante sauce. Serve with tortilla or corn chips.

SO EASY "SHRIMP COCKTAIL" *It doesn't get any easier than this!*

1—8 ounce package cream cheese or Neufchatel (1/3 less fat)

1 small jar seafood cocktail sauce

1 small can tiny shrimp or broken shrimp, drained

- Place unwrapped cheese on plate.
- Top liberally with cocktail sauce, add drained shrimp, and chill.
- Serve with crackers.

DIPS: COLD

REFRIED BEAN DIP

1—15.5 ounce can refried beans

1—4 ounce can chopped green chiles, drained

1 medium tomato, chopped

½ cup sour cream or lite sour cream

2 teaspoons chili powder

¼ teaspoon garlic powder

TOPPING:

½-1 cup shredded Cheddar or Monterey jack or taco cheese

thinly sliced green onion

thinly sliced jalapenos or pickled jalapenos

- Layer the first three ingredients on a serving plate.
- Combine sour cream and spices and add dollops on top of the layered ingredients.
- Scatter topping ingredients on top and serve with corn chips or tortilla chips.

GUACAMOLE DIP *This is my niece Tara Siobhan's recipe.*

2 ripe avocados, peeled and coarsely chopped

2 tablespoons picante sauce

2-3 teaspoons lemon or lime juice

¼ teaspoon chili powder or seasoned salt

- Mash avocados with other ingredients and chill.
- Serve with corn chips or tortilla chips.

ANOTHER IDEA: Leftovers can go on a salad, in a wrap, served along side an omelette, whatever!

GREEN OLIVE DIP *An oft-requested item for "food day" at work!*

1—8 ounce cream cheese or Neufchatel (1/3 less fat)

1—8 ounce package shredded Cheddar cheese

1 cup real mayonnaise (not a blend or sandwich spread or salad dressing for this recipe)

1 small jar pimento-stuffed green olives, drained and coarsely chopped

4 sliced green onions

1 tablespoon lemon juice

½ -1 teaspoon cayenne pepper

- Combine all and chill.
- Serve with corn chips or crackers.

ANOTHER IDEA: I've also used this as a spread for a sandwich wrap. Deli roast beef with chopped romaine lettuce is a winner.

CHILLED ARTICHOKE DIP

1—16 ounce can artichoke hearts, drained and finely minced

½ cup mayonnaise

½ cup sour cream or lite sour cream

¼ cup shredded Parmesan

1 envelope dry Italian dressing mix

- Blend mayo, sour cream, and dry dressing mix.
- Stir in chopped artichokes and Parmesan and chill.
- Serve with thin crackers or flatbread.

DILL DIP FOR VEGETABLES *I like to serve this before a big holiday dinner as folks can keep munching, but not get filled up before the feast.*

1 cup lite sour cream

½ cup lite mayonnaise

1-2 tablespoons chopped fresh chives

2 teaspoons dill weed

1 teaspoon seasoned salt

- Combine all and chill.
- Serve with fresh vegetables: Red, yellow, or green pepper strips, cucumber slices, cherry tomatoes whole or halved, celery sticks, broccoli crowns, cauliflower pieces, halved mushrooms, baby carrots, whatever!

    NOTE: You can buy many of these already cleaned and cut up in the packaged section of the produce cooler at the supermarket or at the salad bar.

ASIAN FLAVORED DIP FOR VEGETABLES

1—8 ounce can sliced water chestnuts, drained and coarsely chopped

1—8 ounce container sour cream or lite sour cream

1 cup mayonnaise or salad dressing blend

¼ cup minced parsley

2 tablespoons minced onion

1 teaspoon soy sauce or lite soy sauce

¼ teaspoon ground ginger

1 clove garlic, minced or one teaspoon from a jar

- Combine all, chill, and serve with fresh vegetables: *See "Dill Dip for Vegetables" for suggestions.*

DIPS: HOT

SWEET ONION CHEESE DIP *Mom was given this recipe when she and Dad retired to Texas thirty-many years ago.*

3 large, coarsely chopped sweet onions such as Vidalia, Walla Walla, or Texas 15's
3-4 tablespoons butter (or margarine if you insist!)
1—8 ounce package shredded Cheddar cheese
1 cup real mayonnaise (not a blend or salad dressing)
½-1 teaspoon bottled hot sauce
1 or 2 cloves fresh garlic, minced or 1 teaspoon if from a jar

- Caramelize the onions and butter in a skillet or in an open foil "pan" on the grill at medium-low or grate over wood fire or in the campfire coals, stirring occasionally.
- When onions are really soft (about 15 minutes), combine with all other ingredients.
- Serve hot with crackers.

HOT NACHOS

1—15.5 ounce can black beans, kidney beans, or chili beans, drained
1—4 ounce can chopped green chiles, drained
2-3 teaspoons taco seasoning mix (or mix 1 teaspoon chili powder, ¼ teaspoon cayenne, dash of onion salt or powder, dash each of salt and black pepper)
2-4 chopped Roma tomatoes or 1 large tomato, chopped and seeded
sliced green onions
sliced jalapenos or pickled jalapenos
1 cup (or more) shredded Cheddar, Monterey jack, or taco cheese

- Combine first three ingredients and spread in skillet or on double thickness foil.
- Top with chopped tomatoes, green onions, and jalapenos.
- Cover and warm in skillet or seal foil and place on medium grill or grate over fire or in hot coals for about 10 minutes.
- Remove cover or open foil pack and top liberally with cheese.
- Serve right out of the skillet or off the foil with tortilla chips.
- Garnish? Sour cream, guacamole, and/or more jalapeno slices or green onion slices.

CHILI CHEESE DIP *This is so simple even my dad (who couldn't even boil water!) could make it!*

1—15 ounce can beef chili without beans
1 can Cheddar cheese soup **or**
1—8 ounce package cream cheese or Neufchatel (1/3 less fat)
1—8 ounce package shredded taco cheese

- Combine in skillet and serve hot with taco chips or tortilla chips.

SALSA

CORN AND BEAN SALSA *Camping buddies Anne and Steve introduced this to us one summer day at Eau Galle Recreation Area near Spring Valley, Wisconsin.*

1—15.5 ounce can black beans, drained
1—15.5 ounce can diced tomatoes, drained
1 cup corn kernels; frozen and thawed or sliced off an ear or two of cooked, leftover corn
   on the cob
1 medium onion, yellow or red, diced
4-5 green onion tops, sliced
1 clove minced garlic or ½ teaspoon if from a jar
juice of 1 lime (about 2 tablespoons if from a bottle)
minced cilantro or parsley (optional)
minced jalapeno (optional)

- Combine all, chill, and serve with scoop-shaped corn chips or tortilla chips.

ANOTHER IDEA: If well-drained, this can be served as a salad or sandwich accompaniment.

TOMATO AND PEPPER SALSA

1--4 ounce can diced green chiles, well drained

2 cups tomato pieces, well drained; can be fresh or canned

1 green and 1 yellow pepper, diced

1 yellow or red onion, diced

1 tablespoon apple cider vinegar; can substitute white vinegar, just not as tasty

½ teaspoon chili powder

½ teaspoon salt

- Combine all, chill, and serve with scoop-shaped corn chips or tortilla chips.

ANOTHER IDEA: If well-drained, this can be served on the side with burgers or as a topper for hot dogs.

PINEAPPLE AND RED PEPPER SALSA *My niece Kari and her hubby Smitty served this with grilled salmon last Easter. Yum! See "Steamed Salmon" in Chapter 5.*

1 cup minced pineapple

½ cup red onion in small dice

½ cup red pepper in small dice

2 tablespoons minced cilantro

2 tablespoons orange juice

OFF THE GRILL

GRILLED BLACKENED CHICKEN WINGS

12 chicken wings, tips removed

2 tablespoons chili powder

2 tablespoons bottled hot sauce if you want these to be "Buffalo Wings"

1 tablespoons blackening spice or

   ¾ teaspoon dried oregano

   ¾ teaspoon cayenne pepper

   ¾ teaspoon garlic salt

   ¾ teaspoon black pepper

   ¾ teaspoon cumin (optional)

commercial bleu cheese dressing or ranch dressing

celery sticks

- Place all ingredients except wings in a one gallon, zipper-style plastic bag.
- Carefully close top, removing as much air as possible, and massage bag to combine.
- Add wings, close, and massage again.
- Oil or spray grill grate and pre-heat to medium heat.
- Grill wings on covered grill about 20 minutes and serve with sour cream, blue cheese dressing, celery sticks, and/or ranch dressing.

GRILLED ZIPPY CHICKEN WINGS

12 chicken wings, tips removed

2 tablespoons lemon juice

1 tablespoon vegetable oil

1 tablespoon Worcestershire sauce

1-2 teaspoons bottled hot sauce

- Marinate and grill as above.

ROASTED GARLIC ON BREAD

2 heads of garlic

1-2 tablespoons olive oil

salt and pepper

sliced French bread, Cuban bread, or baguette

shredded Parmesan cheese (optional)

- Remove papery skin from garlic heads, leaving cloves intact.
- Tip on their sides and lop off the tips with a sharp knife to expose the cloves.
- Place sitting on their bottoms on a double layer of foil.
- Drizzle exposed cloves with olive oil and sprinkle with salt and pepper.
- Seal foil and grill over medium heat or place in hot coals 30 minutes.
- Protecting your fingers with a kitchen towel, open foil and squeeze cooked garlic onto bread slices.
- Top with light sprinkling of Parmesan cheese (optional).

ANOTHER IDEA: Use in "Roasted Garlic Mayo" in "Burger Toppings" in Chapter 4.

GRILLED SHRIMP APPETIZER

1 pound large shrimp, shelled + deveined (You can buy them already shelled and deveined or for less money, you can do it yourself. Use a paring knife to remove the black vein along the back of the shrimp.)

¼ cup lemon juice

¼ cup olive oil

1 teaspoon bottled hot sauce

- Marinate for 30 minutes in a sealed one gallon, zipper-style plastic bag.
- If using wooden skewers, soak skewers 20-30 minutes in water.
- Give all guests 2 wooden skewers and have everyone prepare their own: Thread each shrimp on two parallel skewers to prevent the shrimp from twisting as they grill.
- Grill over hot grill or wood fire or charcoal about 5-6 minutes, turning once.
- Serve with commercial shrimp cocktail sauce or make your own:
  1 cup bottled chili sauce
  2 tablespoons prepared horseradish
  1 tablespoon lemon juice

GRILLED BRIE *This can be served as an appetizer or as a dessert.*

1—15 ounce round of Brie, rind removed

½ cup pecans, chopped

2 tablespoons Kahlua or orange juice

1½ tablespoons brown sugar

2 dollops (meaning "plops"!) orange or apricot marmalade

- Place Brie on double thickness foil long enough to fold over cheese when grilling.
- Combine remaining ingredients and spread on cheese.
- Bring foil loosely over cheese, but not touching the toppings.
- Cover grill and let cook about 15 minutes until Brie is softened.
- If serving as an appetizer: Serve with apple slices and thin crackers.
- If serving as a dessert: Serve with gingersnaps.

BREAKFAST: START THE DAY RIGHT!

EGGS: BASIC EGGS

SKILLET EGGS

- Allow two eggs per person.

- Butter? Non-stick spray? Using butter in the pan will yield extra flavor, but non-stick spray will curb calories and cholesterol.

- Basted eggs? Butter is a must! Spoon melted butter over the yolks and the whites as the eggs cook. Don't break the yolk or turn the egg.

- "Sunny side up"? Just don't break the yolk or turn the egg.

- Scrambled? You don't need to add water, milk, or cream to the eggs when you beat them before cooking. (It's okay if you do, it just thins the eggs. Frugal cooks of old used this "stretch" technique.) Let the eggs cook and use a spatula to move and turn whole swaths of them as they cook---you don't want to end up with "shredded eggs"!

- "Over easy"? Careful! Don't break the yolk as you turn it.

- Fried? Now you want to break the yolk and turn it. Have at it!

- Poached eggs? These are slipped into simmering (not boiling) water to gently simmer until set, meaning the whites are done, but the yolk is still intact and cooked--- yet runny so its rich goodness can ooze over whatever it is placed on like toast or an English muffin or corned beef hash. Break each egg into a cup or onto a saucer and slip it one at a time into the water. Adding a little vinegar to the simmering water will help the eggs stay together in the water instead of becoming "strands" of egg white.

- Omelettes? Just another way to cook scrambled eggs. Allow 3 eggs per omelette. Don't be fooled by their fancy French name: Omelettes start out like scrambled eggs, then are topped with something yummy, and folded in half to finish cooking. (Well, okay, in the end they are *way* prettier than scrambled eggs!)

- Hard-cooked? Often called hard-boiled eggs, these are still-in-the-shell eggs cooked in boiling water or allowed to sit in boiling water long enough that the yolks are completely cooked along with the whites. Easy way: Place eggs in a pan of boiling water, cover, and turn off heat. Let sit 20 minutes and the eggs will be done. Peel and use. Did you know older eggs peel *much* easier than fresher eggs?

Scrambled Eggs
Whipping up a pan of scrambled eggs is the easiest way to do eggs for more than a couple people, and there are so many ways to spark them up. Use these ideas for starters and then get creative!

Each recipe below makes 4 servings at 2 eggs per person, so scramble 8 eggs. Cook as indicated on the preceding page.

DILLED SCRAMBLED EGGS

- Simply shake dried dill weed right out of the spice bottle over the eggs as they cook. Don't confuse dill weed up with dill seed----seed won't be to your liking on eggs!

COTTAGE CHEESE SCRAMBLED EGGS

½ cup cottage cheese added to the beaten eggs before cooking

- Garnish? Any or all: Chopped chives, cheese, crumbled bacon, sprinkled dill weed or seasoned salt.

TACO SCRAMBLED EGGS

½ cup chopped onion, sautéed

½ cup or so shredded Monterey jack cheese or taco cheese

½ cup sour cream

2-3 tablespoons taco sauce

½ teaspoon garlic salt (optional)

TOPPINGS

shredded lettuce

chopped tomato

sliced black olives

shredded cheese

- Sauté onion until soft and leave in skillet.
- Combine all remaining ingredients with 8 eggs and pour over onions.
- Serve with shredded lettuce, chopped tomato, sliced black olives, whatever you would put on a taco.

Omelettes

OMELETTES: THE BASICS

butter

3 eggs

- Add butter to frying pan and let melt *or* spray pan with non-stick spray.
- Scramble 3 eggs with salt and pepper and add to pan.
- Cook on medium without stirring, tilting the pan so the uncooked egg runs off the cooked egg and onto the hot pan.
- When egg looks to be set but still moist, add the filling on one-half and flip the other half over the filling. (Don't worry if you don't get it perfectly on top of the other half.) Another way is to add the filling down the middle and then fold one-third over the filling followed by the remaining third over that.
- Cook until done and tip out onto a plate.

REUBEN OR RACHEL OMELETTE

¼ pound deli corned beef (= Reuben) or turkey (= Rachel). Buy just a few thin slices at the deli or one 3 ounce package and slice into skinny shreds.

small amount of sauerkraut, squeezed to remove liquid

shredded Swiss cheese

1 bottle of commercial 1000 Island dressing

pumpernickel or rye or swirl rye bread for toast

- Filling: Sauté a small amount of the meat with a small amount of sauerkraut and set aside.
- Scramble eggs, pour into pan, and begin to cook until partially set.
- Fill omelette with the sautéed meat and sauerkraut, add a squirt of 1000 Island dressing, and some shredded Swiss cheese.
- Fold and finish cooking.
- Top the now filled-and-folded-in-half omelette with more cheese.
- Serve with 1000 Island dressing (see recipe Chapter 6) on the side and toasted pumpernickel bread.

TACO CHEESE OMELETTE

1 small onion, chopped

Monterey jack or taco cheese

1 teaspoon taco seasoning or 1 tablespoon taco sauce per omelette

butter or non-stick spray

salsa

sour cream

jalapeno slices (optional)

- Filling: Sauté chopped onion with taco seasoning in a little butter or in sprayed pan and set aside.
- Pour eggs in pan and begin to cook until partially set.
- Fill omelette and add ¼ cup of taco cheese or Monterey jack, fold, and finish cooking.
- Top the now filled-and-folded-in-half omelette with more cheese and a couple jalapeno slices.
- Serve with salsa and sour cream.

BLT OMELETTE

2-3 strips of bacon per omelette, fried crisp and crumbled

1 large tomato, seeded and diced

shredded lettuce

mayonnaise or salad dressing blend

- Pour eggs into pan and begin to cook until partially set.
- Fill omelette with bacon and tomato, fold, and finish cooking.
- Top with dollop of mayonnaise and lettuce.

CLASSIC DENVER OMELETTE

diced ham

chopped onion

chopped green pepper

shredded Cheddar cheese

- Filling: Sauté ham, onion, and green pepper until soft and set aside.
- Pour eggs into pan and begin to cook until partially set.
- Fill omelette with ham and vegetable mixture and some shredded cheese.
- Fold, top with more cheese, and finish cooking.
- Serve with classic hash brown potatoes or O'Brien hash browns.

OMELETTES IN A BAG *No pan to wash!*

2 eggs per person

salsa

Various ingredients: Cheese, chopped leftover or fresh veggies like onions, mushrooms, and tomatoes, dill weed, hot sauce, seasoned salt, garlic salt, diced ham, diced peppers or chiles, anything goes! Have ingredients sitting out so diners can select what they want to put in their omelette.

- Hand each diner a one quart, freezer-quality, zipper-top plastic bag and a pen or marker to boldly write his or her name on the bag.
- Have each person assemble their own omelette by putting two eggs in the bag and then selecting desired ingredients from the offerings, placing those into the plastic bag, and sealing carefully, squeezing out as much air as possible.
- Drop 2-4 bags at a time into a pot of boiling water and boil for 10-15 minutes (10 minutes if the bag has fewer ingredients).
- Serve with salsa.

SHRIMP OMELETTE

1 tomato, seeded and minced

1-2 green onions, sliced thinly

chopped parsley

shredded cheese of your choice---try thinly slice Havarti

2-3 cooked shrimp per omelette (Can add shrimp frozen into the skillet.)

- Filling: Warm minced tomato and shrimp briefly in pan and set aside.
- Pour eggs in pan and begin to cook until partially set.
- Fill omelette with sliced green onion, chopped parsley, and shredded cheese or thinly sliced Havarti.
- Fold and finish cooking.
- Top with warmed shrimp, tomato, and more cheese.

MUCHO GRANDE OMELETTE

1—4 ounce can diced green chiles, drained

1-2 tomatoes, seeded and diced

½ pound chorizo or bulk pork sausage, cooked, drained, and crumbled

shredded Monterey jack, cheddar, or taco cheese

sour cream

guacamole

avocado slices

- Pour eggs into pan and begin to cook until partially set.
- Fill omelette with crumbled sausage, tomato, 1 tablespoon minced chiles, and cheese.
- Fold, top with more cheese, and finish cooking.
- Serve with sour cream, salsa, and avocado slices on the side.

SPINACH AND PARMESAN OMELETTE *This is reduced fat meal.*

instead of 3 eggs, use 1 egg and 3 egg whites and ¼ teaspoon salt

fresh or frozen spinach (Buy a handful of fresh leaves at the salad bar, thinly slice, and then chop or thaw 1 package of frozen spinach, squeeze out the liquid, and chop finely, about 2-3 tablespoons per omelette.)

shredded Parmesan cheese, about 2 tablespoons per omelette

bottled hot sauce

- Pour egg mixture into pan and begin to cook until partially set.
- Fill with spinach, 1 tablespoon Parmesan, and a drop or 2 of bottled hot sauce.
- Fold and finish cooking.
- Add ½-1 tablespoon Parmesan on top when served.

CHEESY DILLY OMELETTE

4 ounces cream cheese or Neufchatel (1/3 less fat)

1 tablespoon sour cream or lite sour cream

½ tablespoon minced parsley (optional)

½ teaspoon lemon juice

1/8 teaspoon dried dill weed

1/8 teaspoon garlic powder or garlic salt

dash or 2 black pepper

TOPPING

shredded cheese

minced tomato

green onion slices

- Mix all ingredients except eggs together and warm in small pan or foil pouch on a low heat grill or stove or the side of a wood fire.
- Pour egg mixture into skillet and begin to cook until partially set.
- Fill with warmed cream cheese mixture, fold, and finish cooking.
- Top with a dollop of sour cream when served and shredded Cheddar, minced tomato, and green onion slices.

OATMEAL *Buy "old-fashioned" or "5 minute" oatmeal, not one minute or instant, for improved flavor, fiber, and nutritional value.*

OATMEAL: BASICS
1/3 cup oats to ½ cup water

- Cook in a one gallon, zipper-style, freezer-quality plastic bag --eliminates an ugly, starchy pan to wash!
  NOTE: Don't use a storage bag as the plastic isn't thick enough to withstand the heat.

<u>FOR 4 SERVINGS</u>:
- Place 2 cups dry oatmeal and 1 teaspoon salt in bag. (Salt really is necessary to give the cereal some flavor. It's very blah without it!)
- Add 3 cups boiling water.
- Stir and let stand about 4-5 minutes.

OATMEAL: BEYOND THE BASICS *Oatmeal is a hearty, fiber-filled breakfast choice, but without some "sparks," it can be doggone dull. So, let's spark it up!*

<u>Stir into cooked oatmeal</u>: Applesauce, sweetener of your choice, fresh or dried fruit, nuts, even peanut butter!
  Fresh fruit: Strawberries, blueberries, bananas, peaches, diced apple, kiwi, anything!
  Sweeteners: Brown sugar, honey, white sugar
  Nuts: Walnuts or pecans

<u>Add to bag with boiling water and oatmeal</u>: Dried fruit such as raisins, blueberries, mango, tart cherries, diced apricots, cranberries, diced dates, anything!

<u>Spices</u>: Cinnamon, nutmeg, allspice, pumpkin pie spice, or vanilla extract. Add to cooked oatmeal or put in the bag with the oatmeal and water.

<u>Serve</u>: With milk or half-n-half/coffee cream--half 'n half will make your mouth happy!

FRITTATAS *Frittatas typically start by sautéing vegetables to incorporate into the dish and sometimes include meat as well. (Leftover vegetables from a previous meal make great frittata ingredients!) The sautéed vegetables and meat (if used) are then covered with uncooked, scrambled eggs and cooked until eggs are set. The frittatas here consist of six eggs and make four servings. Cut into 8 wedges and serve 2 per person.*

FAJITA FRITTATA

½ cup sliced or diced onion

sliced peppers: green, yellow, red, as you choose. (Did you know the onions and peppers can be purchased already cleaned, cut up, and ready to cook? Look in the packaged products of the salad cooler at your supermarket or check out the salad bar.)

1 tablespoon vegetable oil, butter, or non-stick spray

½-1 teaspoon chili powder

any leftover steak or chicken from last night? Thinly slice and add to pan.

- Sauté vegetables in oil or butter or sprayed pan.
- Scramble eggs and chili powder in a bowl and pour over all.
- Cook on medium heat about 10 minutes until eggs are cooked.

ITALIANO FRITTATA

½ cup thinly sliced yellow onion

½ cup sliced fresh mushrooms

½ cup sliced zucchini

½ cup sliced or diced green or red pepper

chopped pepperoni—whatever amount you want

1 tablespoon chopped parsley

½ teaspoon dry Italian seasoning or dried oregano or and/basil

1—8 ounce package shredded Mozzarella cheese

1—small jar or can of pizza sauce

- Sauté the sliced vegetables in a bit of butter or sprayed skillet until soft or place in foil pouch and cook on grill or grate over wood fire about 10 minutes or until soft.
- Add pepperoni, parsley, and spices and cook 1-2 minutes.
- Scramble eggs in a bowl and pour over all.
- Cook on medium heat about 10 minutes until eggs are cooked.
- Spoon pizza sauce over all, top with shredded Mozzarella, cover, and let the cheese melt.

MEAT AND POTATOES FRITTATA

2 cups leftover cooked potatoes, sliced or cubed, or hash browns (frozen, fresh, or dehydrated—follow package directions to rehydrate)

1 cup cubed ham (You can buy this already diced or buy a ham steak/center slice and cube enough for this dish and have leftover ham for another meal.)

1 green pepper, chopped

1 tomato, seeded and diced

½ cup sliced fresh mushrooms

1—8 ounce package shredded cheese

bottled hot sauce

seasoned salt

- Fry potatoes in a bit of oil or butter until crisp, turning once.
- Add ham and vegetables and cook 5-6 minutes.
- Mix eggs and add a drop or two of the hot sauce and a couple dashes of seasoned salt.
- Pour over all and cook on medium hear about 10 minutes until eggs are cooked.
- Top with cheese of your choice, cover, and let cheese melt.

EGGS BENEDICT *Who says you can't have a fancy breakfast?? Making Eggs Benny is more work, but if you get everyone to pitch in, it isn't so bad---and you will all be rewarded with a marvelous breakfast!*

Figure on two poached eggs, one toasted English muffin, and two slices of Canadian bacon per person. If you have a "no pork products" diner, consider sautéing one large sea scallop and then splitting it in half horizontally, one half for each muffin half. (Credit to our camping buddy Alan who has been making them this way for years!)

- English muffins, split, toasted, and buttered: Put one person on this task.
- 1 package Canadian bacon slices: Have one person warm these either in a skillet or in foil on the grill or grate. Scallops? Sautéing this ingredient, if used, is also a job for this person.
- 2 packages dry Hollandaise mix plus 1 stick butter: Have another person take charge of making the sauce following directions on package.
- Poach eggs: This is your job as head cook! Once cooked, remove from skillet with slotted spoon or pancake turner to allow the water to run off. See "Poached Eggs" in "Basic Eggs".
- Assemble: English muffin half topped with Canadian bacon or scallop half, followed by one poached egg, and finished off with a generous amount of the Hollandaise sauce and a light sprinkling of paprika if you have it. Serve "open faced."

FRENCH TOAST AND PANCAKES *French toast is simply bread dipped in eggs scrambled with milk and then fried on both sides on a griddle or skillet. Jazz it up by using two slices of bread with a yummy filling (basically making a sandwich) before dipping in the egg. Bask in the warmth of the "ooh's" and "ahh's" of your diners!*

Try using a variety of breads, don't just limit yourself to French bread. Consider cinnamon swirl bread, sourdough bread, Cuban bread, challah, or Texas toast. Also consider trying something more than maple syrup to top the fried toast: Fruit flavored syrups, fruit toppings, jam, butters of all kinds. I've included a few recipes for you to try.

FRENCH TOAST: THE BASICS

2-3 tablespoons butter

sliced bread

2 eggs

¼-½ cup milk or cream (I prefer it to be runnier, so I use more milk.)

1 teaspoon vanilla extract (optional, but it sure adds to the flavor!)

- Melt butter in skillet and pre-heat to medium-hot, just don't let the butter brown. (If it does, remove pan from heat and wipe away the browned butter with a paper towel. You do not want to cook the toast in it.)
- Scramble eggs and milk and pour into a pie pan or other flat container.
- One at a time, dip bread slices in the egg mixture, allowing the excess to drip back into the pan, and place in skillet.
- Fry until nicely browned, about 3 minutes---lift a corner of the bread off the skillet and peek---and flip to cook the other side, again about 3 minutes .
- Peek again to determine if the slice is ready to serve.

PEANUT BUTTER WITH JAM OR HONEY STUFFED FRENCH TOAST *So simple and so sweet!*

peanut butter, chunky or smooth

jam of your choice or honey

- Make a peanut butter and jam/honey sandwich using two slices of the bread.
- Dip in egg mixture and fry as above.

PEANUT BUTTER AND BANANA STUFFED FRENCH TOAST

peanut butter, chunky or smooth

sliced bananas---about ¼ inch thickness or less

cinnamon

- Make a sandwich, either just peanut butter and cinnamon or topped with the sliced banana.
- Dip in egg mixture and fry as above.

ANOTHER IDEA: If you didn't add the bananas to the sandwich, top the fried toast with the fresh slices *or* fry the slices in the skillet as the toast fries, then top the fried toast with the fried bananas. (This is my grandson Jonathan's favorite as the bananas become caramelized and a bit crunchy.)

CREAM CHEESE STUFFED FRENCH TOAST

orange marmalade or other jam/preserves of your choice

cream cheese, softened, or Neufchatel (less fat)

cinnamon

- Spread cream cheese on both pieces of bread.
- Top one cream-cheese-coated slice with the marmalade and make the sandwich.
- Add the cinnamon to the egg mixture, dip sandwiches, and fry as above.

PINEAPPLE AND ORANGE STUFFED FRENCH TOAST *This is a bit more work, so you might want to make the topping ahead of time. Plan to serve it on a lazy morning when you don't have to be running off to something.*

TOPPING:
1--12 ounce jar apricot jam or preserves
½ cup orange juice

FILLING:
1—8 ounce package cream cheese or Neufchatel (1/3 less fat)
1—8 ounce can crushed pineapple, drained (You can add the juice to orange juice for a breakfast beverage.)
½ cup chopped pecans

EGG MIXTURE:
4 large eggs
½ cup milk
½ teaspoon ground ginger
½ teaspoon vanilla extract

- Make topping: Combine jam and juice in a small pan or foil pouch and cook over low-medium heat until combined, stirring frequently. (This can be made ahead of time.)
- Make sandwiches: Combine the cream cheese and ¼ cup crushed pineapple and spread on half the bread slices. Sprinkle with chopped pecans and top with bread slice which has not been spread with cream cheese mixture.
- Make egg mixture: Eggs, milk, ginger, and extract.
- Dip in egg mixture, fry as above, and serve with the apricot orange topping.

ANOTHER IDEA: Simmer the remaining pineapple with ½ cup orange marmalade to make another tasty fruit syrup topping.

Pancakes

Pancakes are a simple, fried dough mixture, usually served with butter and maple syrup. Using a commercial baking mix makes pancakes away from home easy, but you can easily make your own, just takes a few minutes. If making your own pancake mix, do it at home before packing your kitchen bin and be sure to also pack the egg, milk, (buttermilk?), and oil to add at cooking time. If using a commercial mix, be sure to pack whatever ingredients are called for on the box.

BASIC PANCAKE MIX

1¼ cup flour

3 teaspoons baking powder

1 tablespoon sugar

½ teaspoon salt

1 egg

1 cup milk

2 tablespoons vegetable or canola oil

- Combine the dry ingredients in a one gallon, zipper-style plastic bag. (Do this at home if you are making your own pancake mix.)
- Add wet ingredients to the bag and carefully seal top, removing as much air as possible.
- Squish the bag repeatedly until the batter is free of lumps.
- Place the bag in a pan or bowl to give it stability and spoon batter onto skillet. Fry as below in "Basic Pancakes."

BASIC PANCAKES

butter

¼-1/3 cup pancake batter per cake; ¼ cup makes a 4 inch pancake while 1/3 cup makes a six inch pancake. If you want dollar size, measure by tablespoon onto skillet.

- Melt butter in skillet and heat skillet to medium-hot.

  TIPS: #1 Don't let the butter brown. If it does, wipe the skillet with a paper towel and start over.

  #2 Don't let the skillet get too hot or the dough will get crisp edges as it adheres to the melted butter---still edible, but not what a pancake should be.

- Spoon batter onto skillet or use a measuring cup and pour onto skillet.
- Fry until bubbles form all over the cake and the edges begin to look slightly dry.
- Flip and cook the other side until done---use the "peek technique" to check: Lift one side of the cake to see if it's nicely browned.

BLUEBERRY, APPLE, OR CHOCOLATE CHIP PANCAKES

- Add berries, diced apple, or chips to batter **or** sprinkle on each individual cake before flipping. Using the "sprinkle" method is great if you have folks wanting different additions.
- If making apple pancakes, serve with "Applesauce Topping" described below.

SMILEY FACE PANCAKES *Always a kid pleaser!*

- Using a small spoon, drop batter on skillet to approximate eyes and a smile on the finished pancake.
- Let cook a minute before pouring batter over the cooked dough. (The "facial features" will be browner than the pancake when flipped.)
- Flip and cook as usual.

French Toast and Pancake Toppings *Sure, maple syrup (real or imitation) is the granddaddy, but there are so many other ways to serve these. Try something new!*

IMITATION MAPLE SYRUP (AKA "BREAKFAST SYRUP") *Very easy and no high fructose corn syrup! Mom taught me to make this when I was a little girl.*

I cup white sugar or ½ cup white sugar plus ½ cup brown sugar, packed

½ cup water

½ teaspoon bottled maple flavoring. Find in the spice aisle of the supermarket. (This is actually the only ingredient in the whole book which has no other use than making syrup! I owe you an apology.)

- Bring to boil in small pan and cook until all sugar is dissolved.

BLUEBERRY SYRUP *Less expensive than commercial blueberry syrup and no high fructose corn syrup. I have to thank my son's father-in-law Don for showing me this very simple trick.*

1 jar blueberry jam

- Place contents of jar in small pan or foil pouch and heat until runny or remove lid from jam jar and place in a small pan of water and heat until runny.

HONEY PECAN MAPLE SYRUP

1 cup maple syrup or imitation
¼ cup honey
¼ cup chopped pecans
¼ teaspoon cinnamon

- Combine all in small pan or foil pouch and warm.

APPLESAUCE TOPPING

1 cup applesauce
1 tablespoon brown sugar
¼-½ teaspoon cinnamon
dash maple flavoring or maple syrup

- Combine all in small pan or foil pouch and warm.

PEANUT BUTTER AND MAPLE SYRUP *My little grandsons Jonathan and Fletcher LOVE this combo!*

peanut butter

maple syrup

- Spread cooked pancake or French toast with peanut butter.
- Pour maple syrup or imitation over all.

ORANGE SYRUP

I navel orange, peeled and coarsely chopped

I cup maple syrup or imitation maple syrup

I--II ounce can mandarin oranges, drained, and coarsely chopped

- Heat chopped orange pieces and maple syrup in small pan or foil pouch.
- Pour over French toast or pancakes and top with mandarin orange pieces.

PEACHES AND BLUEBERRIES FRUIT COMPOTE *Make this ahead of time and just warm to serve. You can use fresh or frozen fruit.*

I cup sliced peaches, divided

I cup blueberries, divided

2 tablespoons sugar

½ cup water

- Bring ½ cup peaches, ½ cup berries, sugar and water to a boil and simmer gently about 10 minutes.
- Remove from heat and add the remaining fruit.

Flavored Butters *Soften the butter before combining with other ingredients.*

CINNAMON HONEY BUTTER

1 stick butter

1 tablespoon honey

¼ teaspoon cinnamon

CINNAMON MAPLE BUTTER

1 stick butter

1 tablespoon maple syrup or imitation

¼ teaspoon cinnamon

ORANGE BUTTER

1 stick butter

¼ cup orange marmalade

Breakfast Meat and Potatoes

MEATS *Traditional breakfast menus include bacon, fried ham, breakfast sausage links or patties, Canadian bacon for breakfast sandwiches, and grilled sirloin for steak and eggs. Break out of the routine by trying other types of meat such as grilled or fried Kielbasa sausage, cooked and crumbled chorizo sausage, or even shrimp.*

Basic Breakfast Meat Preparation

BACON

- Place slices in a cold skillet and don't overlap slices.
- To prevent grease splatters, fry over medium heat, not hot.
- Turn several times and cook until desired crispness. If using as topping on a dish, fry crisply.
- Remove each slice from skillet when you determine it is done and place on paper plate lined with several thicknesses of paper towel to absorb grease. Cover with more paper towels.

CANADIAN BACON *This just needs to be warmed through. Put it in a skillet, medium low, to warm or wrap in aluminum foil and warm on a grill or on the grate over a wood fire.*

BREAKFAST SAUSAGE LINKS: PORK OR TURKEY

- <u>If cooking in a skillet</u>: Place links in a cold skillet and cook over medium heat several minutes, turning to brown on all sides *or* add 3-4 tablespoons of water to the pan, cover, and cook on medium low without needing to watch them. A couple minutes before you want to serve, remove the lid and any remaining water, and brown the now-cooked sausages.
- <u>If cooking on a grill or wood fire</u>: Skewer links on two parallel skewers so they all turn at the same and can't roll off into the fire. Leave space between links so all sides can brown. Turn 2-3 times.
- *Or* …cut each link into two or three equally sized pieces, give all diners a skewer, and have them skewer and cook their own. If using wooden skewers, be sure to soak in water at least 20 minutes before assembling skewers.

KIELBASA SAUSAGE

- Grill on grill or grate over a wood fire or cook in a skillet over medium heat several minutes, turning to brown on all sides.

HAM

- Place ham steak/center cut slice or pieces in a cold skillet and cook over medium heat several minutes, turning once or grill over medium heat on open grate or on foil, turning once.

SHRIMP

- Skewer on two parallel skewers and grill over hot grill or wood fire about 4-6 minutes, turning once.

Potatoes
Potatoes can be hash browns, fresh fried, or fried leftovers. All want to be served crispy, and this takes time. No shortcuts! Hash browns can be purchased fresh in the dairy case, frozen, or dehydrated. If using dehydrated, follow instructions on the container. Frozen potatoes do not need to be thawed before adding to the skillet.

FRIED POTATOES OR HASH BROWNS *If adding peppers and onions, these are then known as O'Brien Potatoes.*

2 cups hash browns or diced or sliced raw potatoes, peeled or not as you like, or leftover potatoes from last night's dinner. TIP: If you pat them dry with paper towels before adding to the skillet, it will reduce grease splatters.

¼ cup diced onion (optional)

¼ cup diced green and red peppers (optional)

½ stick of butter or ¼ cup vegetable oil

- Melt butter or heat oil in skillet over medium heat.
- Add potatoes, being careful of grease splatters.
- Pat down with spatula to evenly cover the skillet.
- Fry over medium heat about 10 minutes without stirring. (You can cover the pan if you want at this stage.)
- Using a spatula, cut into quarters and flip each quarter to cook the other side. Do not cover at this stage.
- Cook, uncovered, another 10 minutes or so until crisp on both sides.

ANOTHER IDEA: You can jazz these up to suit your menu. Consider adding chili powder, Italian seasoning, dill weed, or seasoned or specialty salt. Or top with cheese.

Breakfast Burritos

PLENTY OF PROTEIN BREAKFAST BURRITOS

1 pound bacon, fried crisply

4—10 inch tortillas, wrapped in foil + warmed on a grill or on grate of wood fire

1—15 ounce can refried beans or reduced fat refried beans

4-6 eggs, scrambled and cooked

shredded Cheddar cheese, Monterey jack, taco cheese, or cheese of choice

hot sauce or salsa

- Warm beans in small pan or foil pouch on grill or over wood fire.
- Have each diner assemble his own burrito: Tortilla, beans, bacon, scrambled eggs, cheese, hot sauce or salsa--whatever he wants!
- Fold one end over ingredients and roll, leaving one end open.

TEXMEX EGG + CHORIZO WRAPS

6—10 inch flour tortillas, wrapped in foil + warmed on a grill or on grate of wood fire

½ pound chorizo sausage, browned, drained, and crumbled

8 eggs, scrambled

2 tablespoons chopped, canned green chiles, drained

1 bottle taco sauce

shredded cheese: Cheddar, Monterey jack, or taco cheese

sliced avocado

- Scramble eggs with green chiles, crumbled sausage, 3 tablespoons taco sauce and cook until done.
- Spoon eggs onto warmed tortillas, top with more taco sauce and cheese.
- Add avocado slices.
- Fold one end over ingredients and roll, leaving one end open.

Breakfast Sandwiches

Breakfast sandwiches are often served on split bagels or toasted English muffins, but consider other breads such as Texas toast, sourdough, or cinnamon bread. These can be toasted on the grill or on a grate over a wood fire. Meats are usually crisply fried bacon, sausage patties, Canadian bacon slices, or ham slices.

BASIC EGG AND MEAT SANDWICH

Basic ingredients per sandwich:

1 egg, fried hard or scrambled

meat of choice, fried or heated in foil or on a skewer over the grill or grate of wood fire

shredded cheese

English muffin split and toasted, bagel split and toasted, or toasted bread

- Prepare ingredients as above and assemble sandwich using both a bottom and a top piece of bread, bagel, or English muffin.

JAZZ IT UP! *Add or subtract any ingredients to make different sandwiches each time.*

- Spread bread item with cream cheese or a light coating of sour cream after toasting.
- Add a slice of fresh tomato or avocado—or both!
- Fry tomato slices in butter before adding to sandwich.
- Have the cheese match the type of menu. Try different cheeses: Parmesan, Havarti or Havarti dill, Swiss, Cheddar, Monterey jack, taco blend, mozzarella, Colby, Muenster, whatever seems to fit your menu.
- Serve open-faced instead of as one sandwich with top and bottom.

Breakfast Sandwiches: No Eggs

HAM AND TOMATO SANDWICH

1—8 ounce package cream cheese or Neufchatel (less fat)

½ cup soft butter

½ cup grated Parmesan cheese

1 teaspoon paprika

½ -1 teaspoon garlic salt

ham slice or deli ham, thinly sliced or shaved

sliced tomato

sliced green onions

English muffins, split and toasted

- Warm ham in skillet or in foil on grill or on grate over wood fire.
- Make cheese spread with first 5 ingredients. *TIP:* If you make this ahead of time, take out of cooler so it comes to room temperature before assembling sandwiches.
- Spread each toasted muffin half with cheese spread, and top bottom half of the prepared muffin halves with sliced green onion.
- Top bottom halves with slice of tomato and warmed ham and top with other muffin half.

SHRIMP SALAD BREAKFAST SANDWICH

1—8 ounce package cooked, frozen small shrimp, thawed or 2—4 ounce cans tiny shrimp, drained

½ cup diced celery

½ cup mayonnaise or salad dressing blend

¼ cup minced onion or sliced green onions

cheese slices

English muffins, split and toasted

- Make shrimp salad with first 4 ingredients. *TIP:* This can be made ahead of time and transported to the site.
- Top half of the toasted muffin halves with shrimp salad and top with a slice of cheese.
- Serve as is or wrap in foil and warm on the grill or over the grate of a wood fire to melt the cheese.

"HOT DOGGIES" BREAKFAST SANDWICHES *Easy and kid friendly!*

1-2 breakfast sausage links per sandwich
shredded Cheddar cheese or American cheese slices
hot dog buns

- Fry or grill sausages.
- Toast split hot dog buns.
- Serve sausage inside the buns topped with cheese. If using sliced cheese, tear into strips and lay in the bun so the entire sausage is cheesy.

Canadian Bacon Sandwiches

#1: WITH CREAM CHEESE AND JAM
Canadian bacon, one slice per sandwich
cream cheese or Neufchatel (less fat)
jam, jelly, or preserves of your choice
English muffins, split and toasted

- Warm Canadian bacon in skillet or in foil on a grill or grate of wood fire.
- Top half of the toasted muffin halves with cream cheese and the other half with jam.
- Add bacon slice.
- Serve as is or wrap in foil and warm on the grill or over the grate of a wood fire to melt the cheese.

#2: BLT

½ cup mayonnaise or salad dressing blend

1 teaspoon dill weed (optional)

Canadian bacon, one slice per sandwich

lettuce: shredded, chopped, or in leaf form

sliced tomato

English muffins or bagels, split and toasted

cheese (optional)

- Combine mayonnaise and dill weed and spread on toasted muffin halves.
- Warm Canadian bacon in skillet or in foil on a grill or grate of wood fire.
- Assemble sandwich: Muffin half, bacon, tomato slice, lettuce, cheese if using cheese, muffin half. If using bagels, serve without top half.
- Serve as is or wrap in foil and warm on the grill or over the grate of a wood fire to melt the cheese.

#3: HOT HONEY MUSTARD BAGELS

commercial hot honey mustard or ½ cup spicy mustard + 2 tablespoons honey

4 slices Canadian bacon, 1 per sandwich

cream cheese

chopped chives or sliced green onion tops

4 bagels, split and toasted or just warmed

- Warm Canadian bacon in skillet or in foil on a grill or grate of wood fire.
- Combine honey and mustard and spread on toasted bagel bottoms.
- Top with bacon, spread cream cheese on bacon, top with chives, and top with other half of bagel if desired or serve open faced.

    TIP: If the cream cheese doesn't melt from the heat of the Canadian bacon, you can wrap the sandwich in foil and place on the grill or grate or in a skillet to melt the cream cheese.

Breakfast Sandwiches with Fruit

BANANA

- Top toasted bread, bagel, or English muffin with cream cheese or peanut butter and add sliced banana.
- Sprinkle with cinnamon or drizzle with honey.

PEANUT BUTTER AND APPLES

½ cup packed brown sugar

½ stick butter, softened

½ teaspoon cinnamon

peanut butter

thinly sliced apple

- Combine sugar, butter, and cinnamon and spread on 1 slice toasted bread, bagel half, or English muffin while still hot from toasting to melt the sweet butter mixture. This will be the top of the sandwich.
- Spread bottom half with peanut butter and top with apple slices.
- Place buttered toast, muffin half, of bagel half on top of apple slices.

APPLE, RAISIN, AND PECAN SANDWICH

1—4 ounce package cream cheese or Neufchatel (1/3 less fat)

2 tablespoons orange juice

2 tablespoons chopped pecans

2 tablespoons raisins, regular or golden

1 tablespoon orange marmalade

dash cinnamon

thinly sliced apple

- Combine all but apple and spread on toasted bagel half, English muffin half, toasted cinnamon bread, or bread of choice.
- Top with apple slices, sprinkle with cinnamon, and top with toasted bread slice or toasted bagel or muffin top.

ANOTHER IDEA: Instead of apple slices, top with well-drained mandarin oranges.

GRILLED CHEDDAR, APPLE, AND BACON *I really like this combination!*

bacon, 2-3 strips per sandwich, crisply fried

thinly sliced apple

white Cheddar cheese (preferred over yellow Cheddar for this sandwich combo)

- Spread toasted bread, bagel, or English muffin with peanut butter, top with apple slices and cheese, and place on foil to make individual pouches.
- Seal loosely so cheese doesn't stick to foil and grill until cheese melts.
- Top with bacon and another slice of bread, bagel top, or English muffin top.

CREAM CHEESE AND FRUIT SPREAD *Really yummy on a warm bagel!*

1—8 ounce package cream cheese or Neufchatel (1/3 less fat) or strawberry cream cheese

1—8 ounce can crushed pineapple, well drained

½ cup (or more) sliced strawberries

bagels, sliced and toasted and still hot

- Combine cream cheese and pineapple.
- Top a hot bagel half with the cheese spread and top off with sliced strawberries.
- Serve open-faced, no top bagel half.

LET'S HAVE LUNCH!

SANDWICHES AND WRAPS *Sandwiches run the gamut from simple to gourmet and everything in between! They are easy to vary, making them a good menu choice when serving people with differing tastes or dietary restrictions such as "no dairy." Experiment with different types of bread and buns: Rye, sourdough, pita pockets, focaccia, multi-grain, sandwich wraps like spinach or whole wheat, tortillas, Kaiser rolls, poppy seed or onion buns, French sandwich rolls, croissants, bagels---there are just so many!*

ITALIAN BREAD + BEEF

1 pound thinly sliced roast beef from the deli

1 pound loaf of unsliced Italian bread

1/4 cup mayonnaise or salad dressing blend

2-3 teaspoons mustard or horseradish

1/4 cup sliced black olives

1/4 cup red onion, thinly sliced

shredded or sliced Swiss cheese

- Slice bread in half horizontally to make a top and a bottom.
- Combine mayo and mustard/horseradish and spread on bread halves.
- Top with beef, olives, onion, and cheese and place top bread half on all.
- Cut into 4 individual sandwiches and serve cold **_or_** wrap each in foil and place on grill or over wood fire to allow cheese to melt.

FRENCH DIP WITH ONIONS AND PROVOLONE *One very tasty sandwich!*

1 pound thinly sliced roast beef from the deli
1-2 large sweet onions, thinly sliced
1-2 tablespoons olive oil or vegetable oil
4 hoagie buns, split horizontally and buttered
seasoned salt or garlic salt
horseradish
Provolone cheese slices
2 packages dry French dip au jus gravy mix

- Cook onion in oil in skillet or foil pouch over medium grill or wood fire until soft, 15-20 minutes. (This can be done ahead of time and then just warmed at lunchtime.)
- Prepare French dip au jus gravy per package instructions and place beef in au jus to warm.
- Spread bun halves with butter, sprinkle with flavored salt, and toast on grill or over wood fire so insides get crunchy.
- Assemble: Bun, beef, onions, cheese, horseradish, bun top.
- Serve with au jus on the side for dipping.

LOTSA MOZZA MEATBALL SANDWICH *Super fast and easy meal!*

½-1 bag frozen meatballs, thawed

1 or 2 -- 26.5 ounce cans spaghetti red sauce

1—1 pound loaf Italian bread, sliced thickly or 4 hoagie rolls or bratwurst buns, sliced in half, but not all the way through the roll. Pluck out some of the bun on the bottom half to make room for the meatballs.

1—8 ounce package shredded mozzarella cheese

- Warm meatballs in red sauce in small pan or foil pouch.
- Make sandwich: Serve as an open-faced, "knife and fork" sandwich by simply spooning over bread slices or spoon into hoagie rolls and add top.
- Top generously with cheese.

HAM SALAD OR HOT DOG SALAD BUNS

hot dog buns, split

½-1 pound sliced ham from the deli, chopped, or cooked, left over hot dogs, chopped

1 cup shredded Cheddar cheese

¼ cup ketchup

2-3 tablespoons mayonnaise or salad dressing blend

Optional: Diced onion, diced olives, diced celery

- Mix all but the buns.
- Stuff buns with meat mixture, wrap each one in foil, and grill or cook over wood fire about 10 minutes, turning once or twice.

HAM CROISSANT OR PITA POCKET SANDWICHES OR WRAPS

4 croissants, split and spread with mayonnaise or salad dressing blend or 4 split and
    halved pitas or one wrap per sandwich
½-1 pound thinly sliced or shaved ham from the deli

- Warm croissant, pita, or wrap by wrapping in foil and placing on grill or above
  wood fire and then spread with mayo when warm.
- Top with any variety: Sliced tomato, lettuce leaf, cucumber slices, avocado slices,
  red onion slices, slice of cheese (Swiss or Havarti?)

HAM AND ASPARAGUS MELT

½ pound cooked asparagus (perhaps left over from last night's meal?)
½-1 pound thinly sliced or shaved ham from the deli
1 slice Provolone cheese per sandwich or other sturdy cheese of choice
sturdy buns such as Kaiser rolls, split
1/3 cup sour cream or lite sour cream
2 tablespoons Dijon mustard
1 teaspoon horseradish

- Combine sour cream, mustard, and horseradish and spread on buns.
- Assemble: Bun, ham, asparagus, cheese, bun top.
- Wrap individually in foil and grill until cheese melts.

ANOTHER IDEA: This also makes a tasty breakfast sandwich.

CRUNCHY PINEAPPLE AND HAM SANDWICH

½-1 pound thinly sliced or shaved ham from the deli

1—8 ounce can pineapple tidbits or crushed + juice---don't drain!

½ —8 ounce package shredded Cheddar or Swiss cheese

½ cup mayonnaise or salad dressing blend

buns or rolls, split

1 cup cole slaw from the deli or make your own. See "Cole Slaw" in salad chapter.

- Combine pineapple, cheese, and mayo and spread on bun bottoms.
- Top with ham and bun top.
- Wrap individually in foil and grill 6-8 minutes.
- Remove from foil and top with cole slaw.

FRESH SPINACH AND BACON SANDWICH

½ pound bacon, crisply fried---this can be done ahead of time.

1—8 ounce package fresh spinach, chopped

bread or buns, toasted, or vegetable wrap, warmed

1/3 cup mayonnaise or salad dressing blend

¼ teaspoon garlic salt or seasoned salt

1-2 drops hot sauce (optional)

- Toast bread or warm wrap by wrapping in foil and placing on grill or above wood fire.
- Combine mayo, salt, and hot sauce and spread on toasted buns or bread.
- Top with bacon slices, chopped spinach, and top half of bun or another slice of bread.

BACON, LETTUCE, AND TOMATO (BLT) *Always my mom's favorite!*

2 slices toasted bread or one vegetable wrap per sandwich

1 pound bacon, crisply fried

1-2 large slices tomato per sandwich

leaf lettuce, iceberg lettuce leaf, or other lettuce per sandwich

mayonnaise or salad dressing blend

- Toast bread on grill or grate or warm wrap by wrapping in foil and placing on grill or above wood fire.
- Assemble on slice of toast or on wrap: Mayo, crumbled bacon or strips, tomato slice, and lettuce. Top with second slice of toast or roll up in wrap.

GRILLED CHEESY PEANUT BUTTER SANDWICH

2 slices bread per sandwich (Try cinnamon bread!)

butter

¾ cup shredded Cheddar cheese

1/3 cup raisins (optional)

1/3 cup peanut butter, chunky or smooth

¼ cup milk

- Combine cheese, peanut butter, milk, and raisins.
- Butter one slice of bread per sandwich and place butter side down in a medium hot skillet or on foil on grill or grate above wood fire.
- Top each slice with one-fourth of the filling and another piece of buttered bread, butter side up.
- Grill until nicely browned, flip, and cook the second side.
- Cut in half on the diagonal.

ANOTHER IDEA: Omit cheese, raisins, and milk. Spread bread with peanut butter, top with jam or jelly, and make a grilled PB + J sandwich.

GRILLED APPLE AND CHEESE SANDWICH

2 slices bread per sandwich

butter

1 cup shredded white Cheddar cheese--nicer with the apple than yellow Cheddar, but you could certainly use yellow.

1 cup diced apple (I like Gala for this sandwich.)

¼ cup minced green olives with pimento (optional)

¼ cup mayonnaise or salad dressing blend

- Combine cheese, apple, olives, and mayo.
- Cook as above for "Grilled Cheesy Peanut Butter Sandwich."

EGG SALAD SANDWICH

6-8 hard-cooked eggs, peeled and chopped coarsely

¼-½ cup diced celery

¼ cup sliced green olives with pimento

¼ cup thinly sliced green onions and tops

¼ cup mayonnaise or salad dressing blend

salt and pepper

- Combine and spread on bread, toast, bagel, whatever.
- Add any of the following: Lettuce leaf, bacon slice, sliced avocado.

CHICKEN SALAD SANDWICH

croissants, pita bread, French rolls, or wrap

2 cups cooked or boiled chicken, canned chicken, or rotisserie chicken

1—8 ounce can crushed pineapple, drained

2/3 cup mayonnaise or salad dressing blend

½ cup shredded carrot (Buy this in a bag in the salad section or at the salad bar of the grocery.)

½ cup peas, frozen (Measure these into a small container or sandwich bag at home and bring frozen to the site. They thaw quickly.)

1 tablespoon lemon juice

salt and pepper

- Stir lemon juice, salt, and pepper into mayonnaise.
- Add to other ingredients and stir to combine.
- Make sandwiches or wraps.

SLOPPY JOES *My son-in-law Mike drools over these!*

4-6 hamburger buns

1 pound ground beef or turkey, browned and drained

1 large onion, chopped and browned with meat

1 slice American cheese per sandwich

1—12 ounce bottle chili sauce

1 cup ketchup

1 tablespoon sugar

1 tablespoon mustard

1 tablespoon Worcestershire sauce

1 tablespoon white vinegar

- Brown meat and onions.
- Add remaining ingredients, cover, and simmer 10-15 minutes.
- Serve on buns with a slice of American cheese.

ANOTHER IDEA: Turn these into Taco Joes by substituting the following for the chili sauce/ketchup mixture to the browned meat and onion:

¾ cup taco sauce or 1 envelope dry taco seasoning

1 tablespoon chili powder (Omit if using the dry seasoning.)

½-1 tablespoon Worcestershire sauce (optional)

PORKY JOES

4-6 hamburger buns

I pound ground pork, browned and drained

I slice American cheese per sandwich

½ cup diced celery, browned with pork

½ cup diced onion, browned with pork and celery

I—10 ¾ ounce can tomato soup

I cup barbecue sauce

- Add soup and BBQ sauce to browned mixture, cover, and simmer 10-15 minutes.
- Serve on buns with a slice of American cheese.

TUNA MELT

2 slices bread per sandwich. (Have you tried wheat bread instead of white?)

2 slices American cheese per sandwich

butter

I—6.5 ounce can of tuna, drained

1/3 cup chopped celery

1/3 cup sweet pickle relish

2 tablespoons mayonnaise or salad dressing blend

sliced tomato

- Combine tuna, celery, relish, and mayo.
- Butter one slice of bread per sandwich and place butter side down in a medium hot skillet or on foil on grill or grate above wood fire.
- Top each slice with one-fourth of the filling, one slice cheese, a tomato slice, a second slice of cheese, and another piece of buttered bread, butter side up.
- Grill until nicely browned, flip, and cook the second side.
- Cut in half on the diagonal.

CRUNCHY TUNA SALAD SANDWICH

sturdy rolls, sliced

1—6.5 ounce can of tuna, drained

½ cup shredded Cheddar or Swiss cheese

1/3 cup mayonnaise or salad dressing blend

¼ cup chopped celery

¼ cup diced water chestnuts (Toss leftovers into a green salad!)

¼ cup chopped green olives with pimento

¼ cup sliced green onion and tops

¼ cup chopped nuts: pecans, cashews, almonds, or peanuts

1 teaspoon Worcestershire

- Combine all but buns.
- Top bun bottoms with one-fourth the tuna mixture and add top bun half.
- Wrap individually in foil and warm on grill or over wood fire until cheese melts.

GRILLED REUBEN OR RACHEL SANDWICH

2 slices rye or swirl rye or pumpernickel bread per sandwich

butter

1 pound thinly sliced corned beef (Reuben) or turkey (Rachel) from the deli

1—15.5 ounce can sauerkraut without caraway, drained and squeezed dry. (You will have some left over.)

1—8 ounce package shredded Swiss cheese or package of slices

1 bottle commercial 1000 Island Dressing or mustard for those who don't like the dressing. See recipe for making your own in the salad chapter.

- Warm meat and sauerkraut in skillet or foil pouch on grill or wood fire.
- Butter one slice of bread per sandwich and place butter side down in a medium hot skillet or on foil on grill or grate above wood fire.
- Top each slice with one-fourth of the warmed meat and kraut, Swiss cheese, and a liberal spread of the 1000 Island or conservative spread of the mustard.
- Top with another piece of buttered bread, butter side up.
- Grill until nicely browned, flip, and cook the second side.
- Cut in half on the diagonal and serve with dill pickles and more dressing or mustard on the side.

GRILLED BBQ CHICKEN WRAP

2 boneless, skinless chicken breasts

1 bottle commercial barbecue sauce

½ bottle commercial Italian dressing

4--10 inch flour tortillas or vegetable wraps

cole slaw from the deli or homemade. See "Cole Slaw" in Chapter 4 Salads.

- Marinate chicken in Italian dressing in 1 gallon, zipper-style plastic bag, up to one hour.
- Grill chicken, medium to medium-high, 6-8 minutes per side, basting with BBQ sauce near the end of the cooking time.
- Wrap tortillas or wraps in foil and warm on the grill or the edge of the wood fire or in a skillet.
- Slice chicken across the grain into 1/8- ¼ inch thick strips.
- Assemble wrap: Chicken strips, cole slaw, more BBQ sauce.

GRILLED CHICKEN CAESAR WRAP

2 boneless, skinless chicken breasts or 2 cups rotisserie chicken, warmed

4--10 inch flour tortillas or vegetable wraps

1 bottle commercial Caesar salad dressing

chopped Romaine

shredded Parmesan cheese

croutons

- Grill chicken, medium to medium-high, 6-8 minutes per side.
- Wrap tortillas or wraps in foil and warm on the grill or the edge of the wood fire or in a skillet.
- Slice chicken across the grain into 1/8- ¼ inch thick strips.
- Assemble wrap: Chicken strips, croutons, Parmesan, and Caesar dressing.
- Slice in half diagonally and serve immediately or the croutons will get soggy.

GRILLED CHICKEN SOUTHWEST WRAP

2 boneless, skinless chicken breasts or 2 cups rotisserie chicken, warmed

4--10 inch flour tortillas or vegetable wraps

salsa

black olives, sliced

cilantro, chopped

sour cream

tomato, chopped

jalapeno slices

avocado slices

shredded lettuce

shredded Parmesan cheese

- Grill chicken, medium to medium-high, 6-8 minutes per side, or if using rotisserie chicken, wrap in foil and warm on the grill or grate.
- Wrap tortillas or wraps in foil and warm on the grill or the edge of the wood fire or in a skillet.
- Slice chicken across the grain into 1/8-¼ inch thick strips.
- Have diners assemble their own wraps.
- Slice in half diagonally.

ASIAN CHICKEN FRUIT WRAPS

2 cups previously grilled chicken breast or rotisserie chicken, warmed

4--10 inch flour tortillas or vegetable wraps, warmed or pita pockets

1—15 ounce can pineapple chunks, drained

1—11 ounce can mandarin oranges, drained

1 cup sliced celery

cashew pieces

1 bottle commercial Asian dressing

- Have diners assemble their own wraps.
- Slice in half diagonally.

ROLL-UPS *These can be made so many ways, it's easy to please 'em all! Use your imagination and get creative! Assemble, slice in half on the diagonal, and chill. Serve cold. See "Burger Toppings" for more spread ideas.*

Wraps: 10 inch flour tortillas, vegetable wraps, or whole wheat wraps. Wrap in foil and warm in skillet, on grill, or over wood fire to make them pliable.

Meats: Crisply fried bacon and thinly sliced or shaved deli meats such as turkey, smoked turkey, ham, beef, chicken, or salami

Cheese: Sliced or shredded Cheddar, American, Swiss, Provolone, mozzarella, Havarti or Havarti dill, Muenster, Monterey jack, taco blend, Parmesan

Veggies: Sliced tomatoes, cucumbers, radishes, green onions and tops, red onion slivers, chopped or sliced olives of any kind, avocado slices, chopped or shredded lettuce, Romaine, or fresh spinach thinly sliced into ribbons

Spreads: Mayonnaise/salad dressing blend, plain cream cheese, Italian dressing, Ranch dressing, or one of these:

Garlic and Herb. Mix 8 ounces cream cheese/Neufchatel with 2 teaspoons minced garlic, 1 teaspoon of Italian seasoning or a mix of dried basil and oregano, dash salt.

Horseradish and Onion. Mix ¾ cup sour cream with ¼ cup sliced green onions or 1-2 tablespoons minced onion, 1 tablespoon horseradish, and 1 teaspoon mustard.

Put That Grill to Work!

ITALIAN SAUSAGES

4 sausages, hot or mild

4 bratwurst buns or hot dog buns, split and toasted

- Prick the sausages with a fork to allow grease to escape while grilling.
- Grill over charcoal, propane, or wood, medium hot heat, about 10-12 minutes, turning frequently.
- Add toppings of choice, and if using cheese, you may want to wrap the sandwich in foil and place over heat to melt cheese.

TOP WITH:

- Pizza sauce and shredded mozzarella cheese or
- Grilled red and green pepper strips or
- Provolone and sliced black olives

BRATWURST *(aka "Brats" pronounced "braaahts", not like a bratty child!)*

4 bratwursts, any variety

4 bratwurst buns or hot dog buns, split and toasted or not

- If the brats aren't pre-cooked: Simmer in a pan of water for 10 minutes or so, being sure to prick the sausages with a fork to allow grease to escape. (Some people prefer to simmer in beer---your choice.)
- Grill over charcoal, propane, or wood, medium hot heat, about 10-12 minutes, turning frequently.
- Add topping and if using cheese, you may want to wrap the sandwich in foil and place over heat to melt cheese.

TOP WITH:

- Sauerkraut or
- Mustard and onions or
- Swiss cheese, onion or sauerkraut, and 1000 Island dressing.

HOT DOGS

good quality hot dogs

hot dog buns

condiments

- Grill hot dogs over medium high heat, about 5-6 minutes, turning frequently and moving around the grill to keep off hot spots.
- Serve in soft buns and top with:
  Plain old ketchup and/or mustard or
  Pickle relish, dill or sweet or
  Shredded cheese, most any variety or
  Mustard and onions or
  Chili and shredded cheese or
  BBQ sauce and cole slaw

Burgers *You can buy patties pre-formed or shape raw ground beef yourself. Shaping them by hand allows you to change the burger from one variety to another by what ingredients you incorporate into the beef---display your creative side! You also have the opportunity for portion control by making four burgers per pound vs. three or even making the smaller slider sized patties.*

BURGER BASICS

- Grill over medium hot heat 7-8 minutes before flipping to cook the other side. If you have really thick burgers, then cook 9-10 minutes per side. Sliders? 5-6 minutes per side.
- If you smash the burgers or flatten with a spatula, you will lose flavor carried by the juices you just pushed out of the burger.
- Toasted buns add a nice texture. Try different types like Kaiser buns, onion buns, rye buns, sesame or poppy seed topped, or ciabatta rolls.

SUPER MOIST HAMBURGERS *My pal Judy-Ann taught me this one years ago.*

1 pound ground beef
1-2 tablespoons soy sauce
buns

- Combine, shape, and grill as above.

HORSERADISH CHEESEBURGERS

1 pound ground beef
3 tablespoons prepared horseradish
1 tablespoon Worcestershire sauce
1 cheese slice per burger or "Cheese Spread for Burgers." See "Burger Toppings."
buns

- Combine all but cheese and shape into patties.
- Grill and after flipping, top with cheese.

TACO BURGERS

1 pound ground beef

1 envelope dry taco seasoning

avocado slices

salsa

buns

- Mix beef and seasoning and form into patties.
- Grill, top with Monterey jack cheese.
- Serve topped with a slice of avocado with salsa on the side.

PINEAPPLE TERIYAKI BURGERS

1 pound ground beef

1—8 ounce can pineapple slices with juice (1 tablespoon juice goes in the meat mixture; pour the rest into orange juice for a breakfast beverage.)

¼ cup teriyaki sauce. You can buy this or make your own. (This is wonderful, by the way):

  2 tablespoons soy sauce

  2 tablespoons honey

  2 cloves minced garlic

  1 teaspoon salt

  ¼ teaspoon ground ginger

lettuce

mayonnaise or salad dressing blend

buns

- Add 1 tablespoon of the pineapple juice and the teriyaki sauce to meat.
- Mix, shape, and grill.
- Grill one pineapple slice per burger, turning once, until grill marks appear.
- Serve on toasted buns: Burger, pineapple slice, lettuce, mayo

ANOTHER IDEA: Omit pineapple juice and add 1 clove minced garlic, a couple sliced green onions, and some diced water chestnuts to the beef. Baste burgers and pineapple slices with teriyaki sauce as they cook.

BLACKENED BURGERS *I like to serve these as "sliders" as they pack a lot of punch. You can find slider-sized buns in the commercial bread aisle.*

Sprinkle blackening spice mix on both sides of each patty. You can find this in the spice aisle or make your own:

1 tablespoon paprika

1 tablespoon chili powder

1 teaspoon garlic powder or garlic salt

1 teaspoon onion powder (optional)

Couple dashes each: black pepper and cayenne

- Grill 5-7 minutes per side, depending on the size of the burger.

Suggestion: Serve with "Dill Pickle Mayo" or "Lemon Mayo." See "Burger Toppings."

STUFFED CHEESEBURGER (AKA "JUICY LUCY")

1 American cheese slice per burger or other cheese of choice

2 thin ground beef patties per sandwich

buns

condiments

- Fold the cheese into a square and place on the middle of one patty.
- Top with the second patty and crimp the edges with a fork to make one "filled" burger.
- Grill, being careful when you turn it not to break the patty and lose the cheese.
- Serve with dill pickles, lettuce, sliced tomato, sliced onion, whatever you like on a cheeseburger or "Green Onion Mayo." See "Burger Toppings."

GARLIC, MUSTARD, AND GRILLED PEPPER BURGERS

1 pound ground beef
3 tablespoons mustard or Dijon mustard
4 cloves minced garlic
grilled red pepper strips
olive oil or vegetable oil
buns

- Combine beef with mustard and garlic and shape into patties.
- Grill pepper strips while grilling burgers: Toss strips with oil before placing on grill.
  TIP: To avoid losing pepper strips through the grate, make an aluminum foil "pan" with one inch sides, slice the bottom several times to allow the flames to caress the peppers, and grill the peppers in this "pan".

ANOTHER IDEA: Instead of the pepper strips, grill some sweet onion slices to top your burgers. Thinly slice 2 sweet onions like Vidalia's, Walla Walla's, or Texas 15's, toss with oil, and grill about 15 minutes, tossing occasionally.

PIZZA BURGERS *Spray or oil your grill as these will stick.*

1 pound ground beef
1/2 -1 pound bulk pork sausage
1 jar or can pizza sauce, separated
onion slices, thinly sliced
grated Parmesan cheese
1 slice Mozzarella cheese per burger or shredded
buns, toasted

- Combine beef, pork, and 2 tablespoons pizza sauce and shape into 6-8 patties.
- Spray grill and grill one side, flip, top each with a spoonful of pizza sauce, one onion slice, and cheese.
- Serve on toasted bun and top bun.

ANOTHER IDEA: Add any other pizza style toppings you like such as sliced olives or pepperoni.

Burger Toppings

What you top your burger with can make all the difference between "OK" and "WOW!" Many of the following are equally great as a spread for a sandwich or wrap or even as a dip for fresh vegetables or as a topping for cooked vegetables.

- Combine ingredients and let sit for at least 10 minutes to allow flavors to meld.

GARLIC DILL MAYO

1 cup mayonnaise or salad dressing blend

2 cloves minced garlic

1 tablespoon lemon juice

2 teaspoons fresh minced dill or dried dill weed

couple dashes each: salt and pepper

GREEN ONION MAYO

½ cup mayonnaise or salad dressing blend

½ cup sliced green onions and tops

1-2 teaspoons hot sauce

couple dashes sugar

LEMON MAYO

½ cup mayonnaise or salad dressing blend

1 tablespoon lemon juice

DILL PICKLE MAYO *This is one of my all-time favorites! Great with Blackened Burgers. See recipe in this chapter.*

½ cup mayonnaise or salad dressing blend

¼ cup dill pickle relish, squeezed almost dry

I tablespoon Dijon mustard

¼ teaspoon paprika

ROASTED GARLIC MAYO

I head of roasted garlic, mashed. See "Roasted Garlic on Bread" in Chapter I.

I cup mayonnaise

juice of I lemon (about 3 tablespoons if from a bottle)

TANGY MAYO

½ cup mayonnaise or salad dressing blend

¾-I teaspoon paprika

I/2 teaspoon minced garlic from a jar or one fresh clove minced

I/2 teaspoon lemon juice

¼ teaspoon cayenne

dash of salt

dash of sugar

HORSERADISH MAYO

½ cup mayonnaise or salad dressing blend

1-2 tablespoons prepared horseradish

2 teaspoons lemon juice

2 teaspoons chopped chives, fresh or dried or flash frozen (optional)

1 teaspoon minced garlic

dash salt

dash cayenne

HORSERADISH SOUR CREAM

½ cup sour cream or lite sour cream

2-3 tablespoons prepared horseradish

1 tablespoon prepared mustard

sliced green onions

PIMENTO CHEESE SPREAD *Makes an absolutely fabulous cheeseburger!*

½ cup shredded Cheddar cheese
¼ cup cream cheese or Neufchatel (1/3 less fat)
2—ounce jar pimentos, drained and chopped

ANOTHER IDEA: Add ¼ cup mayonnaise or salad dressing blend to above plus couple dashes salt and cayenne.

AND ANOTHER GREAT IDEA: Add the drained and chopped pimentos to the ground beef before shaping into patties.

SPICY KETCHUP *Make this as hot as you want!*

2/3 cup commercial ketchup
2 tablespoons strong mustard
1 tablespoon honey
1 tablespoon Worcestershire sauce
2-3 teaspoons bottled hot sauce
chopped jalapeno or pickled jalapenos

SIMPLE, SAVORY SOUPS

Hot soup is so welcome on cool days, so add these to your outdoor cooking repertoire for the days when it's not hot and humid. All use simple ingredients and come together fast. Your diners won't believe you didn't slave over a simmering pot all day!

QUICK VEGGIE SOUP *So easy and so good for you!*

1—46 ounce can vegetable juice

1—16 ounce package frozen mixed vegetables

1—one ounce envelope dry onion soup mix

- Combine and simmer about 15-20 minutes.
- Add some pasta or rice if you want a heartier soup.

EASY CORN CHOWDER

1—15.5 ounce can whole kernel corn, drained or 2 cups corn kernels cut off leftover corn-on-the-cob plus "juice" from scraping the empty cobs

1—10 ¾ ounce can cream of potato soup

1 1/3 cup milk

1 tablespoon butter

- Combine and simmer 15-20 minutes.
- Top with sliced green onion tops, chives, or crumbled crisp bacon.

SAUERKRAUT SOUP *Also called "German Sausage and Potato Soup"---so re-named by my college friend Helen because her hubby Perry insists he doesn't like sauerkraut---but loves this soup!*

I ring smoked sausage, cut into ¼ inch "coins" and then halved or quartered

I—24 ounce package sauerkraut, drained a bit yet retaining over half the juice

4-6 potatoes, peeled and diced into bite-sized pieces or smaller

8 cups good quality beef broth (not bouillon!)

shredded Swiss cheese----don't skip this! It's essential to the flavor.

- Combine all but cheese and simmer 15-20 minutes until the potatoes are done.
- Top with shredded Swiss cheese and pass extra cheese to add individually.

QUICK TORTILLA SOUP

2—10 ¾ ounce cans chicken and rice soup

I—15.5 ounce can diced tomatoes with green chiles and juice

6—6 inch corn tortillas, sliced thinly and then into bite-sized pieces

leftover chicken

shredded cheese: Cheddar, Monterey jack, Mexi-blend, or taco

- Combine canned soup, tomatoes, and tortilla pieces and simmer 15 minutes.
- Add chicken and top with shredded cheese.

CHEESY POTATO AND HAM CHOWDER

1—15.5 ounce creamed corn and liquid

1—10 ¾ ounce can Cheddar cheese soup

2 cups frozen hash browns

1-2 cups diced ham (Buy already diced from the deli or buy a ham steak/center cut ham slice and dice it yourself. You'll have enough left to make another dish or add to a salad or scrambled eggs.)

1 carrot, sliced thinly or shredded (This is just for color, so leave it out if you don't want to fuss with it.)

- Bring to boil and simmer 15 minutes: Hash browns, carrot, and 2½ cups water.
- Add and heat through: Corn, canned soup, ham, plus ½ cup water.

NEW ENGLAND STYLE CLAM CHOWDER *This one is kinda spendy, but it's sooo worth it!*

2—10 ounce bottles clam juice (Look in the juice section of the supermarket.)

2 medium potatoes, peeled and diced into small pieces

1 medium onion, diced

1 carrot, peeled and diced or shredded (Carrots are just for color, so leave out if you want to.)

1 stalk celery, thinly sliced (optional)

1—6.5 ounce can tiny shrimp, drained

1—6.5 ounce can minced clams, drained

1 cup half 'n half coffee cream or whipping cream or heavy cream

chopped parsley

crisp, crumbled bacon

oyster crackers

- Combine first 5 ingredients, cover, and simmer 20 minutes.
- Add, cover, and heat through: Seafood and cream.
- Garnish with chopped parsley and crumbled bacon and serve with oyster crackers.

CHILI—BASIC RECIPE

1 pound ground beef or turkey, browned and drained

1 medium onion, diced and browned with beef/turkey

1—16 ounce can tomato pieces and liquid

1—10 ounce can tomato pieces with green chiles and liquid

2—15.5 ounce cans beans: Chili beans and gravy or kidney beans (light or dark) with liquid

1—15.5 ounce can tomato sauce

1 envelope dry chili seasoning or 1 tablespoon chili powder, ½ teaspoon cumin, and ½ teaspoon cayenne

- Brown ground beef/turkey and onion.
- Add the rest, cover, and simmer 20 minutes.
- Garnish? Sour cream, shredded Cheddar or Monterey jack or Mexi-blend, or sliced green onions. Serve with cornbread muffins, corn chips, or saltines.
- Feeling creative? Add chopped peppers of any variety, chipotle powder, cinnamon, chocolate, black beans, or whatever you dream up to add color and heat!

SALADS

Chicken

"Store bought" chicken salad will taste incredibly "blah" after enjoying one of these fresh salads! Chicken salad can be easily made from rotisserie chicken, grilled leftover chicken breasts, canned chicken, or plain boiled chicken. It can be served by itself, in a hollowed-out tomato, on a bed of lettuce, or in a wrap as a sandwich.

CHICKEN SALAD WITH GRAPES

2-3 cups cooked chicken, cubed

1 cup green or red grapes or a combination, cut in half

½ cup sliced celery

½ cup mayonnaise or salad dressing blend

¼ cup sour cream or lite sour cream

¼ cup minced onion

1 tablespoon lemon juice

½ teaspoon salt

- Make dressing by combining mayo, sour cream, lemon juice, and salt.
- Combine with remaining ingredients and chill.

ANOTHER IDEA: You can "punch up" this dish by adding chopped water chestnuts, sweet pickle relish or diced sweet pickles, chopped hard-cooked egg, pineapple tidbits, or chopped olives.

APRICOT CHICKEN SALAD

2-3 cups cooked chicken, cubed

½ cup almonds, toasted, or salted cashews

½ cup sliced celery

½ cup diced dried apricots

DRESSING

½ cup plain yogurt

¼ cup mayonnaise or salad dressing blend

3 tablespoons apricot preserves or jam

½ teaspoon ground ginger

½ teaspoon salt

- Make dressing.
- Combine with remaining ingredients and chill.

ASIAN CHICKEN SALAD *So easy and so tasty!*

2-3 cups cooked chicken, cubed

1—11 ounce can mandarin oranges, drained

1—10 ounce bag chopped Romaine or other greens

½ -1 cup frozen snow peas

¼ - ½ cup slivered almonds, preferably toasted

chow mein noodles

commercial Asian sesame salad dressing

- Combine all but chow mein noodles and Romaine.
- Serve on greens and top with chow mein noodles.

SANTA FE CHICKEN SALAD

2-3 chicken breasts

one envelope dry taco seasoning

1 cup commercial Ranch dressing

2 tablespoons minced onion

2 tablespoons minced tomato

¾ teaspoon paprika

1—10 ounce bag chopped Romaine or iceberg lettuce

shredded cheese: Cheddar, Monterey jack, taco, Mexi-blend

1 bag taco chips or commercial tortilla strips

sour cream

guacamole

pico de gallo, commercial or make this easy version:

    1 large tomato, diced and seeded

    ½ cup diced onion

    ¼ cup chopped cilantro or parsley

    ¼ cup lime juice

    2 cloves garlic, minced or 1 teaspoon if from a jar

    ¼ teaspoon salt

    jalapenos, diced (optional)

- Toss chicken in taco seasoning and grill medium high, 4-7 minutes per side, depending on thickness.
- Let rest a few minutes before slicing thinly across the grain.
- Make dressing: Combine ranch dressing, onion, tomato, and paprika.
- Place lettuce on each plate and top with dressing, crunched taco chips or tortilla strips, cheese, chicken strips, pico de gallo, sour cream, and guacamole.

Beef *Beef can be grilled steak, deli roast beef, or browned ground beef---or even leftover prime rib from a doggie bag!*

SOUTHWESTERN BEEF SALAD

½ pound deli roast beef in thin cut (but not shaved or it will just fall apart), sliced into
    ¼ inch strips or thinly sliced leftover steak

1—10 ounce bag chopped lettuce or Romaine or other greens

1—8 ounce bag shredded Monterey jack cheese

1—2.25 ounce can sliced black olives, drained

2 large tomatoes cut into 8-12 wedges

1 small onion cut into thin slices and separated into rings

tortilla chips or commercial tortilla strips

DRESSING

1—8 ounce container sour cream or lite sour cream

½ cup commercial French salad dressing

1 teaspoon chili powder

- Make dressing.
- Place lettuce on plates and top with tomato wedges, onion rings, olives, and beef strips.
- Spoon dressing over all and top off with crunched-up tortilla chips or tortilla strips.

TACO SALAD *Supper in a flash if you cook the beef at home and just warm it at the site.*

1 pound ground beef, browned

1 package dry taco seasoning

1—10 ounce bag chopped Romaine or other greens

1—10 ounce can kidney beans, drained

1—2.25 ounce can sliced black olives, drained

shredded cheese: Cheddar, Monterey jack, taco, or Mexi-blend

diced onion

sour cream

guacamole

taco chips or tortilla chips, crunched-up when adding to salad

salsa or picante or commercial Western salad dressing or make this:

    1 cup 1000 Island salad dressing

    ½ cup sugar

    1 tablespoon commercial taco sauce

    1 tablespoon taco seasoning

- Brown beef and then simmer in taco seasoning and water per package directions. TIP: If making at home, securely wrap seasoned ground beef in foil and warm at the site on grill or grate over wood fire while assembling the rest of the salad.
- Let everyone make their own salad by layering ingredients of choice, starting with a base of Romaine.

Turkey

SMOKED TURKEY *Deli smoked turkey, baby spinach, and walnuts make a very nutritious and delicious meal!*

1 pound deli smoked turkey cut into ¼ inch slices and then cut in half
1—10 ounce package baby spinach
4 green onions, sliced
½ cup walnut pieces
½ cup vegetable oil
¼ cup red wine vinegar
1 teaspoon seasoned salt
1 teaspoon dried Italian seasoning or ½ teaspoon each basil and oregano
couple dashes pepper

- Make dressing: Combine oil, vinegar, seasoning, and spices.
- Toss dressing with turkey, onions, and walnuts in one gallon, zipper-style plastic bag and chill.
- Serve over spinach bed.

Tuna

TUNA SPAGHETTI SALAD *This is easier to "make and take" due to its need to be served cold. Therefore, it makes a great first night supper on a weekend so it doesn't have to take up cooler space that long.*

8 ounces spaghetti, broken into 3 inch pieces when tossed into boiling water to cook

2—5 ounce cans tuna, drained and flaked

4 tomatoes, chopped and seeded

¼ cup chopped fresh basil

¼ cup chopped fresh parsley

¼ cup mayonnaise or salad dressing blend

¼ cup commercial Caesar salad dressing

1 tablespoon fresh oregano or 1 teaspoon dried oregano

- Cook spaghetti per package directions and drain.
- Combine mayo and Caesar dressing.
- Combine all and chill. Serve cold.

Pasta

CHEESE TORTELLINI SALAD *This pasta salad is served cold and is another great "make and take" entrée.*

2—9 ounce packages cheese tortellini (Find in the grocery's cooler section.)
1—6 ounce jar marinated artichoke hearts, drained and chopped
1 tomato, chopped and seeded
¼ cup chopped fresh parsley
¼ cup grated Parmesan cheese plus more to pass

- Cook the tortellini per package directions and drain.
- Toss with cheese, allowing cheese to melt.
- Toss with all other ingredients and chill.
- Serve with extra cheese on the side.

Slaw *When thinking of "slaw" most folks conjure up cole slaw, a vegetable salad made with shredded cabbage. That's not the only kind---see my mother's recipe for sweet onion slaw below.*

PICKLED SWEET ONION SLAW *Mom was given this recipe when she and Dad retired to Kerrville, Texas, over 30 years ago. This is another good "make and take" recipe due to the need to be refrigerated while marinating.*

3 sweet onions such as Vidalia, Texas 10-15's, or Walla Walla, sliced thinly
¼ cup white vinegar
¼ cup sugar
¼ cup water
¼ cup mayonnaise or salad dressing blend
1/8 teaspoon celery salt

- Marinate onion slices 8 hours in vinegar, sugar, and water in refrigerator.
- Drain, rinse, and pat dry with paper toweling to remove the taste of the brine.
- Combine mayo and celery salt and stir into onions.
- Serve chilled.

VEGETABLE SLAW *This makes a lot, so you may want to cut it down.*

1—1 pound cole slaw mix
2 cups diced tomatoes, seeded
1 cup chopped broccoli crowns
1 cup chopped cauliflower crowns
½ cup chopped purple or red onion
¼ cup mayonnaise or salad dressing blend
¼ cup sour cream or lite sour cream
1 tablespoon white vinegar
1 teaspoon salt
couple dashes pepper

- Make dressing: Combine mayo, sour cream, vinegar, salt and pepper.
- Toss all and chill.

GERMAN HOT BACON SLAW *This harkens back to my German great-grandmother, but she had to shred the cabbage herself, just as she did when making sauerkraut.*

1 package cole slaw mix
¼ cup chopped onion
½ pound bacon, fried crisp and crumbled, bacon drippings reserved
2 tablespoons cider vinegar
1 teaspoon sugar

- Cook vinegar and sugar in bacon drippings until combined.
- Pour over cole slaw mix and onions.
- Top with bacon and serve hot.

24-HOUR COLE SLAW *Very economical! Make a day ahead. It will shrink as it sits.*

1—1 pound bag cole slaw mix or one head shredded cabbage, about 8 cups
½ cup shredded carrot (Buy it already shredded.)
1¼ cup mayonnaise or salad dressing blend
3 tablespoons white vinegar
3 tablespoons sugar
2 tablespoons milk, half 'n half coffee cream, or whipping cream
3-4 dashes salt

- Combine all and chill overnight.

ANOTHER IDEA: You can add various additional ingredients to tailor the slaw to your menu or just change it up: Chopped parsley, drained crushed pineapple, sliced green onions, or sweet pickle relish.

CREAMY SLAW *Horseradish adds a nice bite!*

½ of a 1 pound bag cole slaw mix
1 tablespoon chopped fresh parsley
½ an apple, chopped but not peeled
¼ cup mayonnaise or salad dressing blend
2 tablespoons cider vinegar
2 tablespoons sugar
2 teaspoons prepared horseradish
salt and pepper

- Combine all and chill 30 minutes.

"SORT OF TEXMEX" COLE SLAW

1—1 pound bag cole slaw mix

DRESSING

½ cup mayonnaise or salad dressing blend

¼ cup chopped fresh chives or dried or freeze-dried

3 tablespoons lime juice

2 tablespoons chopped fresh cilantro

2 tablespoons honey

1 teaspoon salt

1/8 teaspoon cayenne

- Combine all but vegetables.
- Toss with vegetables and chill.

MANY FLAVORED SLAW

1—1 pound bag cole slaw mix

1—11 ounce can mandarin oranges, drained

½ cup shredded carrot (Purchase in the vegetable department or salad bar.)

¼ cup raisins (Plump in boiling water if they are dried out and tired looking.)

¼ cup sunflower kernels

1 small container orange flavored yogurt

- Combine all and chill.

ANOTHER IDEA: Change this into a fruit slaw by subbing halved grapes and a chopped apple instead of the carrot and raisins above.

MARINATED CAULIFLOWER SLAW *This is another favorite of mine!*

½ head cauliflower, flowerets cut into ¼ inch slices

1 stalk celery and leaves, diced

4-5 green onions and tops, sliced

DRESSING

1 cup mayonnaise or salad dressing blend

3 tablespoons cider vinegar

1 clove garlic, minced or ½ teaspoon if from a jar

2-3 dashes hot sauce

- Toss all and chill.

RAMEN NOODLE SLAW *This is another "Food Day" favorite of my work group. Shelly always brings this salad and we love her for it!*

1—1 pound package cole slaw mix

1—3 ounce package ramen noodles with chicken flavor packet

½ cup sunflower kernels

½ cup slivered almonds

3-4 sliced green onions and tops

½ cup vegetable oil

1/3 cup sugar

1/3 cup cider or white vinegar

- Shake in a tightly covered container to make the dressing: Oil, sugar, vinegar, and contents of flavor packet.
- Just before serving, crunch up the noodles in the bag, add to other ingredients, and toss with dressing.

Vegetable Salads

Salads made with greens or spinach do not hold well once dressed, so only toss what you think will be eaten at the meal. Or serve without dressing and let folks top their own salads.

HOMEMADE DRESSINGS *"Really," you ask, "in this day and age?" Well, yes! They're fast, very economical, and you don't have a plastic or glass bottle to add to the trash or haul to recycle. So…why not try a homemade dressing?*

CREAMY LEMON PARMESAN DRESSING *Great on greens of any kind!*

¼ cup sour cream

2 tablespoons lemon juice

1 tablespoon grated Parmesan cheese

1 teaspoon Dijon mustard

RED WINE VINEGAR VINAIGRETTE

¼ cup lemon juice

2 tablespoons red wine vinegar

2 tablespoons olive oil

1 tablespoon honey

salt and pepper to taste

- Whisk or use a fork to combine all but olive oil.
- Drizzle in olive oil while stirring constantly.
- Season to taste with salt and pepper.

WHITE WINE VINEGAR VINAIGRETTE

2 tablespoons white wine vinegar

2 tablespoons thinly sliced green onion

1 ½ tablespoons lemon juice

1 tablespoon olive oil

1 tablespoon Dijon mustard

1 teaspoon honey

salt and pepper to taste

- Shake in a tightly covered container.
- Season to taste with salt and pepper.

GARLICKY VINAIGRETTE

2 tablespoons olive oil

1 tablespoon red wine vinegar

1 teaspoon Dijon mustard

1-2 cloves garlic, minced, or ½-1 teaspoon if from a jar

¼ teaspoon salt

1/8 teaspoon pepper

- Shake in a tightly covered container.

1000 ISLAND DRESSING

½ cup mayonnaise or salad dressing blend

1 tablespoon ketchup

1 tablespoon bottled chili sauce or shrimp cocktail sauce

1 tablespoon sweet pickle relish

1 teaspoon lemon juice

1 teaspoon prepared horseradish

salt and pepper to taste

- Stir vigorously with a fork.
- Season to taste with salt and pepper.

Fresh Vegetable Salads *A little of this, a little of that, toss, and serve! You can find many of the ingredients already cleaned and cut up for you in the salad section of the grocery or at the salad bar—just buy what you need, no muss, no fuss, no waste.*

BROCCOLI CAULIFLOWER SALAD *This has color and zip!*

1-2 cups cauliflower flowerets, sliced

1-2 cups broccoli flowerets, sliced

4 green onions and green tops, sliced

3-4 radishes, sliced

½ -1 cucumber, sliced

DRESSING

1 cup mayonnaise or salad dressing blend

2 tablespoons white wine vinegar

1 tablespoon sugar

1 teaspoon salt

1 clove garlic, minced, or ½ teaspoon if from a jar

- Combine and shake dressing ingredients in a tightly covered container and toss with vegetables.

ITALIAN BROCCOLI SALAD *Make as much or as little as you need.*

broccoli flowerets
pepperoni, sliced thinly and quartered
olives, green or black or a combination, sliced
shredded or diced Swiss cheese
commercial ranch or Italian dressing.

- Toss all.

ANOTHER IDEA: Add cooked spiral pasta and turn this into a main dish salad.

BROCCOLI, CAULIFLOWER, AND TOMATO SALAD

1 cup broccoli flowerets, broken up
1 cup cauliflower flowerets, broken up
1 tomato, chopped and seeded
2 green onions and tops, sliced

DRESSING
¼ cup sour cream or lite sour cream
¼ cup mayonnaise or salad dressing blend
salt and pepper

- Combine sour cream and mayo, season to taste with salt and pepper, and toss with vegetables.

ANOTHER IDEA: This could easily become a main dish salad by adding cooked spiral pasta and diced pepperoni, salami, or ham.

CHEESE AND BROCCOLI SALAD

2 cups broccoli flowerets, sliced

¾ cup Cheddar cheese with salami, diced (With salami is really nice, but if you can't find it, just use regular Cheddar.)

¼ cup sunflower kernels

6 green onions and tops, thinly sliced

DRESSING

½ cup sour cream or lite sour cream

½ cup mayonnaise or salad dressing blend

2 teaspoons red wine vinegar

salt and pepper

- Combine sour cream, mayo, vinegar, season to taste with salt and pepper, and toss all.

CRUNCHY VEGETABLE SALAD *This one is always a hit!*

1—10 ounce bag Romaine pieces or other greens

1—8 ounce can sliced water chestnuts, drained

1 cup salted cashew pieces

¼ cup sunflower kernels

1-2 bunches green onions and tops, sliced

chow mein noodles

DRESSING

½ cup vegetable oil

½ cup sugar

½ cup apple cider vinegar

1 teaspoon salt

- Combine oil, sugar, vinegar, and spices in a tightly covered container. Chill until serving time, shaking occasionally.
- Toss salad at serving time and top with chow mein noodles.

MANDARIN TOSSED SALAD *Make the dressing or use commercial Asian sesame dressing.*

1—11 ounce can mandarin oranges, drained
1—10 ounce bag Romaine pieces or other greens
1 tablespoon sunflower kernels
3-4 green onions and tops, sliced

DRESSING
3 tablespoons vegetable oil
2 tablespoons sugar
2 tablespoons cider vinegar
1 tablespoon orange juice concentrate
2 teaspoons red wine vinegar

- Make dressing by placing oil, sugar, OJ, and vinegars in a tightly sealed container. Add enough water to make 1 cup, cover securely, and shake vigorously to blend.
- Toss with salad ingredients above.

FOUR LAYER SALAD *Reminiscent of the old Seven Layer Salad served at church suppers during my youth.*

1 head iceberg lettuce, torn, or one bag of lettuce or other greens
½ of 1—16 ounce bag of frozen green peas, thawed
1 red or purple onion, chopped
1 cup shredded or diced Swiss cheese
mayonnaise or salad dressing blend or commercial Ranch dressing
crisply fried bacon for garnish

- Layer greens, peas, onion, and cheese in serving dish and top with mayonnaise, salad dressing blend, or Ranch dressing.

SUMMER "ANYTHING ON HAND" SALAD

any vegetables at the Farmer's Market or in your garden: Broccoli, carrots, cauliflower, celery, cucumbers, onions, peppers, radishes, tomatoes, yellow squash, zucchini, and anything else on hand such as olives or mushrooms

any fresh fruit on hand

commercial dressing of choice or shake vigorously in tightly covered container:

    1 cup mayonnaise or salad dressing blend

    ¼ cup horseradish

    ¼ cup sugar

    1 teaspoon salt

    1 teaspoon pepper

- Assemble chosen veggies and fruits, cleaned and sliced or diced and toss all.

ITALIAN TOMATO AND CHEESE SALAD

1—4 ounce can sliced black olives, drained

1 large tomato, seeded and diced

1-2 cucumbers, seeded and sliced

1 medium to small zucchini, sliced

1 purple onion, thinly sliced

1 cup Mozzarella cheese cubes

1 bottle commercial Italian dressing or Ranch dressing

- Toss all and chill.

AVOCADO AND TOMATO SALAD

1—4 ounce can sliced black olives, drained

2 avocados, peeled and diced

1-2 large tomatoes diced or substitute cherry tomatoes cut in half

½ head lettuce or bagged lettuce or Romaine or other greens

diced onion

DRESSING

1/3 cup Thousand Island dressing

1 teaspoon chili powder

- Combine dressing and chili powder and toss.

ANOTHER IDEA: Instead of dressing as above, squeeze 2 limes over all, sprinkle with salt or kosher salt, and drizzle with a bit of olive oil while tossing.

CUCUMBERS IN DILLED SOUR CREAM *My grandmother taught me to serve cucumbers like this, and I've been enjoying them this way for many years.*

1 large cucumber or English cucumber, seeded and sliced ¼ inch thick and then sliced in half to make half-moons

3 tablespoons mayo

3 tablespoons sour cream or lite sour cream

3 tablespoons red onion, minced

2 tablespoons white wine vinegar

2 tablespoons salt

1 tablespoon chopped fresh dill or 2 teaspoons dried dill weed

- Cover cucumber slices with salt and let sit 15-20 minutes to bring the moisture out of the cucumber.
- Rinse off brine and pat dry with paper toweling.
- Combine remaining ingredients and pour over cucumber slices.
- Let sit a few minutes before serving.

ORANGE AND ONION SALAD *The ingredients may sound strange together, but this is really tasty!*

1 orange, peeled, sectioned, and sections cut in half
1 small purple onion, thinly sliced
¼ cup olive oil or vegetable oil
¼ cup red wine vinegar
2 tablespoons minced fresh parsley
salt to taste
lettuce, romaine, or other greens

- Combine oil, vinegar, parsley, and salt in a tightly covered container and shake to combine. Chill.
- Serve orange sections and onion slices over greens and dress with dressing.

PINEAPPLE GREEN SALAD *So easy---no chopping!*

1—8 ounce can pineapple tidbits, drained and juice/syrup reserved
salad greens of choice
1 cup shredded green or red cabbage (Buy already shredded.)
¼ cup mayonnaise or salad dressing blend
2 tablespoons reserved pineapple juice/syrup

- Combine juice and mayo and toss.

ANOTHER IDEA: Use 2 tablespoons frozen orange juice concentrate, thawed, instead of the pineapple juice.

GRILLED POTATO SALAD *No potatoes to peel! No boiling!*

4-5 small "B" sized red potatoes per person, scrubbed and cut in half but not peeled
1 small onion, chopped
2 tablespoons butter
salt and pepper
commercial Ranch dressing
sliced green onions and tops
crisply fried bacon for garnish (optional)
hard cooked egg slices for garnish (optional)

- Place potatoes and chopped onion on a double thickness of aluminum foil with enough extra foil to make a packet with a bit of air space.
- Dot with butter and add salt and pepper before sealing packet.
- Place on medium-low to medium heat and cook 20-25 minutes until potatoes are easily pierced. You'll begin to smell them as they near the end of the cooking time.
- Serve out of foil pack and let each diner top her own with dressing, green onion slices, egg slices, and bacon.

ANOTHER IDEA: If you have leftovers, fry them in a skillet for breakfast the next day.

GRILLED SWEET POTATO SALAD *This is good served hot or cold.*

3 sweet potatoes, peeled and cubed
2 apples with green skin (Granny Smith maybe?), in dice or thin slice, with peel
4-5 green onions and tops, sliced
commercial poppy seed dressing

- Place potatoes on a double thickness of aluminum foil with enough extra foil to make a packet. Seal, leaving a bit of air space.
- Place on medium-low to medium heat and grill about 15 minutes until potatoes are easily pierced.
- Open packet and allow to cool while you cut up the apples and green onions.
- Toss all and serve.

SPINACH SALADS *Buy bagged or salad bar baby spinach. If baby spinach is not available, tear pieces in half or quarters and remove most of the stems.*

APPLE AND SPINACH SALAD

1—10 ounce bag spinach

2 hard-cooked eggs, sliced

1 red apple, diced, with peel

3-4 green onions and tops, sliced

½ cup shredded Cheddar cheese

½ cup mayonnaise or salad dressing blend

½ cup sour cream

bleu cheese (optional)

crisply fried, crumbled bacon for garnish

- Combine mayo and sour cream.
- Toss just before serving and garnish with bleu cheese and bacon.

ANOTHER IDEA: Instead of sour cream, substitute ¼ cup frozen orange juice concentrate, thawed but not diluted. Or swap out the apple with a small can of drained pineapple tidbits.

STRAWBERRIES AND SPINACH SALAD *So good when the berries just come on the market!*

1—10 ounce bag spinach

1 cup strawberry halves

1 cup pecan pieces. Better when toasted in skillet or on foil on grill until just fragrant.

½ cup red onion slices, sliced very thinly and separated into rings

commercial poppy seed dressing

- Combine all.

GARDEN SPINACH SALAD

1—10 ounce bag spinach

1 cup shredded Cheddar cheese

2 large tomatoes, diced

1 cup sliced or diced celery

¼ cup sunflower kernels

mayo and sour cream as in "Apple and Spinach Salad" above or commercial Ranch
    dressing

Fruit Salads and Dressings

CREAMY ORANGE DRESSING

1—8 ounce package cream cheese or Neufchatel (1/3 less fat)

1/3 cup sugar

¼ cup orange juice

1 teaspoon vanilla extract (optional)

ANOTHER IDEA: Using pineapple juice in place of the orange juice is really good,
too.

HONEY MAYONNAISE

½ cup mayonnaise

1½ tablespoons honey

ORANGE YOGURT

I container orange yogurt or I container vanilla yogurt

2 tablespoons orange marmalade

FRESH FRUIT SALAD *Good with any of the above dressings.*

I red apple, thinly sliced

I peach, peeled and sliced

I pear, thinly sliced

I cup green grapes, halved

2 kiwi fruits, peeled and sliced

¼ cup pecan pieces (optional)

JUST PEACHY FRUIT SALAD *This makes a lot and is an easy dish to make and take. There is no dressing--the peach pie filling binds the salad.*

I—2I ounce can peach pie filling

I—20 ounce can pineapple chunks, drained

I—II ounce can mandarin oranges, drained

strawberries: I container fresh berries sliced or I container frozen sliced strawberries, thawed

I banana

- Combine all but banana and chill.
- When ready to serve, slice a fresh banana over the top and gently fold in.

APPLE AND ORANGE

1 red apple, chopped

1 cup green grapes, halved

1 cup diced celery

1 recipe "Orange Yogurt" or "Creamy Orange Dressing" above

RUMMY WATERMELON SALAD

cubed seedless watermelon

<u>DRESSING</u>

½ cup sugar

1/3 cup rum

3 tablespoons lime juice

- Combine sugar, rum, and lime juice and shake in a tightly closed container.
- Pour over watermelon and chill.

Pasta Side Salads *Best made before as a "make and take" item since these are served chilled.*

BACON, LETTUCE, AND TOMATO "BLT" SALAD *My friend Melissa often brings this for "Food Day" at work and shared her recipe with me.*

1 pound good quality bacon, fried crisp and crumbled

1 pound box bow-tie pasta, cooked, rinsed, and drained

2 tomatoes, diced and seeded

½ head iceberg lettuce or 1—10 ounce bag chopped iceberg or Romaine

¾ cup (or to taste) mayonnaise or salad dressing blend

salt

- Combine all and chill.

PRETTY PASTA SALAD

½ --16 ounce box rotini, cooked, rinsed, and drained

2 cups cherry tomatoes, halved

1 cup chopped cucumber or English cucumber

½ cup chopped celery

2-3 green onions and tops, sliced

Provolone cheese, cut into strips and then halved

bottled commercial Italian or Ranch dressing or mayonnaise or salad dressing blend

- Toss selected dressing with ingredients, cover, and chill.
- Toss again at serving time.

SUPPERTIME

Grilled French Bread
Or use Italian, Vienna, or Cuban, unsliced. Buy a one pound loaf of bread or equivalent, split in half horizontally or cut into individual slices. Spread with filling, wrap in foil, and grill until warmed through.

DILLY BREAD

¼ cup butter

¼ cup shredded or grated Parmesan

1/8 cup finely chopped fresh dill or 1 tablespoon dried dill weed

2 cloves garlic, minced or 2 teaspoons if from a jar

ITALIAN CHEESY BREAD

3 tablespoons olive oil

½ cup grated Romano/Romano Parmegiano cheese

fresh cracked pepper or ½ teaspoon from a can

HERBED GARLIC BREAD

½ cup butter

¼ cup grated or shredded Parmesan cheese

2 cloves garlic, minced or 2 teaspoons if from a jar

¼ teaspoon oregano

CHEESY GARLIC BREAD

1—8 ounce package shredded cheese: Mexican blend, Cheddar, taco blend, whatever you like

¾ cup mayonnaise or salad dressing blend

¼ teaspoon garlic salt

Rolls

GRILLED CHEESE ROLLS

6 dinner rolls, split

1—8 ounce package cream cheese or Neufchatel (1/3 less fat)

½ cup shredded Cheddar cheese

¼ cup sliced green onions and tops

1 tablespoon milk

2 teaspoons Dijon mustard

- Combine all ingredients except the rolls.
- Spread on roll bottoms and re-place roll tops.
- Wrap all of them in one foil packet and grill over slow coals or slow heat, 10 minutes or until cheese melts.

PIZZA ON THE GRILL *We often plan on these for the first night of the weekend as everyone can make their own whenever they get to the site---and there are no pans to wash. I prefer to use commercial, pre-baked, individual-sized crusts rather than fresh pizza dough when I am not making these on my larger grill at home.*

1 individual-sized pizza crust per person or fresh pizza dough

commercial pizza sauce and/or commercial alfredo sauce

toppings of choice: pepperoni, artichoke hearts, pineapple, Canadian bacon, onions, peppers, olives (green and/or black), sauerkraut, sausage or hamburger (cooked at home so it's ready when you get to the site), ham, sliced mushrooms, dill pickles, sliced jalapenos, the sky's the limit!

shredded cheese: mozzarella, Cheddar, Monterey jack, Mexi-blend, again whatever you want for the type of pizza you are making

- If doing individual-size pizzas: Have each diner assemble his/her own pizza, advising them not to pile the ingredients too deep or the pizza won't get warmed through.
- Cook on pre-heated grill, low to medium low, or in skillet on low heat until cheese is melted. If the heat is too high, the crust will burn and blackened crust is just not that tasty.

LEMON PARMESAN ANGEL HAIR PASTA

8 ounces angel hair pasta, cooked at site or earlier at home and then frozen in a one gallon, zipper-style freezer quality plastic bag and then placed into a large pot of boiling water at the site for about 10-15 minutes until thawed and hot. (Use the hot water later for washing dishes.)

¼ cup good quality shredded Parmesan cheese

1 tablespoon olive oil

2 teaspoons lemon zest (You can find this in jars in the spice aisle at the grocery or you can scrape a fresh lemon with a fork at the site.)

salt and pepper to taste

- Toss all and pass the Parm.

SKILLET HAM AND ASPARAGUS WITH SPIRAL PASTA *This may look like a lot of bother, but it really isn't. It comes together pretty fast.*

2 cups spiral pasta cooked at site or earlier at home and then frozen in a one gallon, zipper-style freezer plastic bag and then placed into a large pot of boiling water at the site for about 15-20 minutes until thawed and hot. (Use the hot water later for washing dishes.)

¾ cup fresh asparagus, cut into 1 inch pieces

1 tablespoon olive oil or vegetable oil

1 yellow pepper, seeded, and cut into skinny strips and then cut those in half

1 zucchini, sliced and slices cut in half

½ pound cubed ham (You can buy this pre-packaged in the meat department, get it in the deli, or dice half of a center cut ham slice and have the other half left over for breakfast.)

5 tomatoes, diced

¼ cup shredded Parmesan cheese

¼ cup minced parsley

1 teaspoon Italian seasoning or ½ teaspoon each: dried oregano + dried basil

½ teaspoon salt

¼ teaspoon cayenne

- Sauté asparagus and pepper in oil in skillet until tender.
- Add tomatoes and ham and heat through.
- Toss with hot pasta and zucchini.
- Mix parsley and spices and toss with pasta, vegetables, and ham.
- Plate each meal and pass shredded Parmesan as topping.

SKILLET CIDER TENDERLOIN *Nice with mashed potatoes.*

1 pork tenderloin, sliced into 1 inch pieces

1 tablespoon olive oil or vegetable oil

1 cup apple cider

½ cup white wine

1 tablespoon apple cider vinegar

- Heat oil in skillet, add pork slices and brown on both sides, about 3-4 minutes per side.
- Add apple cider, wine, and vinegar, cover, and bring to boil.
- Remove lid, reduce heat to medium, and simmer about 5 minutes, turning slices two times.
- Remove pork and let sauce continue to cook down another 8-10 minutes.
- Serve reduced sauce over pork slices and mashed potatoes.

SPICY CHICKEN OVER NOODLES

4 cups egg noodles, cooked at site or earlier at home and then frozen in one or two one-gallon, zipper-style freezer plastic bags and then placed into a large pot of boiling water at the site for about 10-15 minutes until thawed and hot. (Use the hot water later for washing dishes.)

1 pound chicken tenders, sliced into ½ -1 inch pieces

1—15 ounce can tomato sauce

1—14.5 ounce can diced tomatoes, drained

1 green pepper, seeded cut into thin strips

1 onion, chopped

2 cloves garlic, minced, or 1 teaspoon if from a jar

1 tablespoon olive oil or vegetable oil

2 teaspoons chili powder

couple dashes salt and sugar

- Sauté in oil about 4-5 minutes until the juices in the chicken run clear: Chicken, pepper strips, onion, garlic.
- Add, bring to boil, reduce heat, and cook uncovered 6-8 minutes: Tomato sauce, drained tomatoes, and spices.
- Serve over noodles.

ANOTHER IDEA: This could also be served over cooked rice.

SUPER EASY CHICKEN BURRITOS

1—10 ounce can refried beans

1 ¼ cup cooked chicken (leftovers or rotisserie?)

8-inch flour tortillas, wrapped in foil and warmed on grill, grate over wood fire, or in
skillet

1 envelope dry taco seasoning

shredded cheese: Mexi-blend, Cheddar, Monterey jack, taco

diced tomato

thinly sliced onions or green onion

salsa

- Shake chicken in a bag with the taco seasoning.
- Assemble burritos with ingredients of choice, wrap each in foil, and place seam side up on heat source.
- Heat 10-15 minutes until everything is heated through.
- Top with cheese and serve with salsa.

KIELBASA SAUSAGE AND PINTO BEANS *Filled with protein + quick to the table.*

1 pound Kielbasa, sliced thinly

1 large onion, chopped

1 green pepper, seeded and chopped

1—15 ounce can pinto beans, drained

1—14.5 ounce can stewed tomatoes with liquid

1—10 ounce can diced tomatoes and chiles with liquid

1—8 ounce can tomato sauce

1 tablespoon vegetable oil

½ teaspoon garlic powder

- Sauté onion and pepper in oil about 4-5 minutes.
- Add the rest, bring to boil, reduce heat, and cook gently about 10 minutes.

SKILLET PORK CHOPS WITH GRAVY *These were my brother Lew's favorite, God rest his soul. Serve with boiled or mashed potatoes.*

2-4 chops
1—10.5 ounce can cream of mushroom soup
½ can milk
1 envelope dry onion soup mix
1 tablespoon vegetable oil

- Brown chops on both sides in oil.
- Mix soups and milk and pour over chops.
- Cover and cook on medium low about 20 minutes.

CREAMY SKILLET PORK CHOPS AND POTATOES
2-4 chops
2 sliced onions
1—10.5 ounce can cream of potato soup
1 cup sour cream or lite sour cream
thinly sliced raw potatoes or 1-2 cans potatoes, drained
1 tablespoon vegetable oil

- Brown chops in oil on both sides and remove from pan if using raw potatoes.
- Add raw potato slices to pan and top with chops and onion slices. If using canned potatoes, place them on top of the chops and onions.
- Spoon soup over all, cover, and cook on medium low about 20 minutes.
- Uncover, spoon sour cream over all and simmer about 5-6 minutes.

MONGOLIAN BEEF *Cook in skillet and serve with rice.*

I pound sirloin or flank steak, cut thinly against the grain. TIP: Did you know that it is
a lot easier to slice raw meat if the meat is still a bit frozen?

I ½ tablespoons cornstarch

I tablespoon oil

3 cloves garlic, minced, or 3 teaspoons if from a jar

1/3 cup soy sauce

1/3 cup brown sugar

½ teaspoon ground ginger

sliced green onions for topping

- Heat oil in skillet.
- Toss beef strips with cornstarch and add to skillet.
- Stir-fry beef, garlic, and ginger until beef appears cooked through.
- Add ½ cup water, the soy sauce, and the brown sugar.
- Cook, stirring, 3-4 minutes.
- Serve with rice and top with green onions.

SKILLET BEEFY BEAN CASSEROLE *This is my cousin Dale's wife Gayle's time-tested recipe.*

I pound ground beef

I large onion, diced

I—28 ounce can pork and beans and liquid, but toss out that glob of fat

I—15 ounce can kidney beans, drained

I—15 ounce can butter beans, drained

$\frac{1}{2}$ cup ketchup

$\frac{1}{4}$ cup packed brown sugar

I tablespoon yellow mustard

I tablespoon cider vinegar

- Brown ground beef and onion.
- Add the rest and gently combine.
- Cover and cook on medium low about 15-20 minutes.
- If it's too soupy, serve it as a soup if your troops are starving right now or uncover and let it cook down another 10 minutes or so.

SKILLET POOR MAN'S CHOW MEIN *I grew up on this casserole, so you know this is a very old recipe!*

I pound ground beef or turkey

3 large onions, chopped

4-5 stalks celery, sliced, and roughly chopped

I—10.5 can cream of mushroom soup

$3\frac{1}{2}$ cups boiling water

I cup raw white rice

$\frac{1}{4}$ cup soy sauce

I tablespoon packed brown sugar

1-2 cloves garlic, minced, or I teaspoon if from a jar

chow mein noodles

- Brown ground beef, onion, and celery.
- Add remaining ingredients.
- Stir, cover, and cook on medium low about 25 minutes.
- Serve over crisp chow mein noodles and pass the soy sauce.

SKILLET MEXICAN BEEF CASSEROLE *Super quick meal!*

1 package tortilla chips

1 pound ground beef

1 large onion, diced

2 cups shredded cheese: Mexi-blend, Cheddar, Monterey jack, taco, whatever

2 cloves garlic, minced, or 1 teaspoon if from a jar

1—10.5 can cream of mushroom soup

1—10 ounce can or jar enchilada sauce

1—4 ounce can diced green chiles, drained

- Brown ground beef, onion, and garlic.
- Add soup over all and sprinkle with chilies.
- Top with enchilada sauce and cheese.
- Cover and cook on medium about 8 minutes, just until warmed through.
- Serve and pass tortilla chips to crumble on top for crunch.

ANOTHER IDEA: When warmed through, place on warmed tortilla and roll up.

SKILLET SHRIMP SCAMPI *Fancy? Yes! Easy? Yes! Yummy? Yes!*

1-2 pounds small shrimp, peeled and deveined

loaf of French bread to sop up that marvelous garlic butter!

1 stick butter (No short cuts! Real butter is a must for this dish.)

¼ cup minced onion

4 cloves garlic, crushed or 2 teaspoons if from a jar

1-2 tablespoons minced parsley

¼ cup dry white wine

2 tablespoons lemon juice

- Melt butter in skillet and sauté garlic and parsley about one minute.
- Add shrimp, continue to cook about 3-4 minutes until shrimp turn pink, and remove shrimp into dish and keep warm by covering the dish completely with a clean, heavy towel.
- Add wine and lemon juice to butter mix in skillet and cook about 2 minutes before pouring over shrimp.
- Serve in bowls with slices of French bread.

SKILLET STIR-FRY *Stir-fry is a fast way to put a nutritious meal together. Simplify the process by buying bags of frozen stir-fry vegetables, so no cleaning or chopping raw vegetables to do. Purchased fortune cookies would be a fun ending to this meal!*

1 cup raw white rice cooked at home and frozen in a one quart, zipper-style freezer-quality plastic bag

½ pound chicken strips or "tenders" cut into bite-sized pieces or ½ pound sirloin cut into thin strips across the grain and then cut in half

1 tablespoon cornstarch

½ cup water

¼ cup soy sauce

2 teaspoons vegetable oil

prepped vegetables: Any assortment of sliced mushrooms, halved cherry tomatoes, small broccoli pieces, thinly sliced carrot, water chestnuts from a can (drained), pepper slices (green, yellow, or red), onion slices, small pieces of cauliflower buds, green onions in ½ inch slice, whatever!

- Heat 3 cups water in a large pan, bring to a boil, and add bag of cooked rice. Keep boiling and remove rice with a tongs at serving time. (Use hot water to wash dishes.)
- Shake cornstarch, soy sauce, and water in tightly covered container and set aside.
- Stir-fry chicken or sirloin in hot oil in skillet until it appears cooked, about 3-4 minutes.
- Push to sides of skillet and add vegetables, stirring as they cook.
- When vegetable all appear to be cooked to "crisp tender", shake cornstarch mixture and stir it in, bringing to boil and cooking and stirring one minute.
- Serve over cooked white rice.

Beef *Beef grilled over charcoal or wood has so much more flavor than when grilled over gas or pan-fried in a skillet. If using a wood fire, it is really helpful to have a grill basket of some kind to place the meat in---particularly welcome when it comes time to flip the steak! If using a propane grill, consider using a drip pan with a layer or two of soaked wood chips under the meat to help give that smoky flavor to the beef.*

BASIC STEAK

WHAT TYPE OF BEEF? Sirloin, rib eye, filet, flank steak, T-bone, porterhouse, New York strip, whatever you like---figure 1/3 pound per person when purchasing if without bone; ½ pound per person if bone in.

SHOULD IT BE MARINATED? Marinate or not, that's up to you---and the cost of the beef! Please don't even think of marinating a filet---that would just be a waste given all the natural beef flavor in that cut! If not marinating, consider rubbing the steak with olive oil before placing on the grill or in the skillet.

WHAT TEMPERATURE TO COOK ON? Pre-heat grill or skillet so it is hot enough to sear the meat when first placed on the surface. Some people believe in cooking the entire time on high, and some turn the fire down once the beef sears on one side. Try both methods and adopt the one that works for you.

WHAT ABOUT GRILL MARKS? To get those attractive grill marks on a steak, turn it 90 degrees after the first minute on the grill. The cooking term for these marks is "quadralage" (QUAD-ra-lahzz) which is just plain fun to say!

HOW LONG TO COOK IT? Well, that depends on the thickness of the steak and how well you like it done---rare, medium rare, medium, or shoe leather. For a ¾ inch cut, start with 5 minutes per side. If not done to your liking, put it back over the fire or back into the skillet. You can always cook it longer, but if you overcook it, there's no taking that back.

WHAT'S WITH "RESTING TIME"? Always allow a few minutes for the steak to rest after removing from the cooking surface. This lets the juices settle back into the meat and flavor the beef.

Marinades

Combine all ingredients in a one gallon, zipper-style plastic bag. Squeeze out all air, seal, and massage bag to mix. Add meat, poultry, fish, whatever, and let marinate in cooler at least half an hour; longer is fine, just be sure to keep it chilled. If you want to baste the beef while grilling, reserve some of the marinade before adding the beef to it. Never re-use any marinade which has had raw meat in it.

NOTE: *Flank steak can (and may need to) marinate overnight.*

BROWN SUGAR AND GARLIC *This has been my personal favorite for years.*

½ cup packed brown sugar

¼ cup olive oil or vegetable oil

¼ cup cider vinegar

¼ cup lemon juice

2-3 tablespoons grainy mustard

½ tablespoon salt

6 cloves fresh garlic, minced, or 2 tablespoons if from a jar

WOOSTA AND WINE VINEGAR *This is pretty basic—and pretty tasty, too!*

½ cup Worcestershire sauce

¼ cup olive oil or vegetable oil

2 tablespoons red wine vinegar; can sub another type of vinegar, but I have found the red wine variety gives just the right "tang". (Red wine vinegar is a workhorse in my kitchen!)

1 tablespoon minced garlic

PINEAPPLE AND SOY SAUCE *I like to use this one on sirloin and beef kabobs.*

½ cup soy sauce

¼ cup packed brown sugar

¼ cup pineapple juice

¼ cup white wine vinegar or white vinegar

½ teaspoon garlic salt

TERIYAKI FLAVOR *This is also wonderful on chicken breasts and chicken kabobs.*

½ cup vegetable oil

½ cup red wine vinegar

¼ cup teriyaki sauce

2 tablespoons Worcestershire sauce

2 teaspoons dry mustard

3-4 shakes black pepper

1 clove garlic, minced, or 1 teaspoon from a jar

BEEF FAJITAS MARINADE

¼ cup vegetable oil

¼ cup red wine vinegar

1 teaspoon sugar

1 teaspoon chili powder

1 teaspoon garlic salt

1 teaspoon dried oregano (optional)

SHERRY AND SOY SAUCE

1/3 cup dry sherry

1/3 cup soy sauce

2 tablespoons chopped green onion and tops

2 teaspoons Dijon mustard

couple dashes ground ginger

generous amount of black pepper

Spreads and Sauces

HERBED GARLIC BUTTER *This is great on grilled bread or corn on the cob, too!*

1 stick soft butter

1 tablespoon chopped parsley

1 tablespoon lemon juice

¼ teaspoon garlic salt

HERB CHEESE LOG

1—8 ounce package cream cheese, softened, or Neufchatel (1/3 less fat)

3 tablespoons thinly sliced green onions and tops

2 teaspoons lemon juice

2 teaspoons minced chives, fresh or bottled

2 teaspoons basil, sliced very thinly and minced if fresh

- Shape into a log on a piece of plastic wrap, seal, and chill.

HORSERADISH SAUCE *Nice bite!*

3/8 cup prepared horseradish

¼ cup sour cream or lite sour cream

1 tablespoon finely chopped chives

HORSERADISH CREAM REDUCTION SAUCE *Easy and oh-sooo-good!!*

1½ cups chilled whipping cream

3 tablespoons prepared horseradish

1/8 teaspoon salt

1/8 teaspoon pepper

- Heat cream in pan, medium low heat, until reduced in half.
- Add remaining ingredients and continue to heat on low a couple minutes to let flavors meld.

Entrees

GRILLED FLANK STEAK WITH SHERRY SAUCE

1 recipe "Sherry and Soy Sauce" marinade

1½ pounds flank steak

8 ounce carton plain, low fat yogurt

2-3 tablespoons sliced green onions and tops

2 tablespoons dry sherry

2 teaspoons Dijon mustard

- Marinate steak 8 hours.
- Mix up the sherry sauce and chill at least 1 hour before serving: Yogurt, green onions, sherry, and mustard.
- Grill steak, medium, 6-8 minutes per side.

BEEF FAJITAS

1 recipe "Beef Fajitas Marinade." See recipe in this chapter.

1½ pounds sirloin or flank steak

2 onions, sliced thinly

2 red peppers, cut into strips

1 green pepper, cut into strips

¼ cup olive oil

flour tortillas

toppings of choice: Picante, salsa, guacamole, green onions, shredded cheese, sour cream.

- Reserve some marinade before adding beef.
- Marinade 1½ pounds sirloin in fajita marinade 2 hours or if using flank steak, marinate 8 hours or overnight.
- Grill meat, basting with marinade, medium heat, turning once until done to your liking. Let rest 3-4 minutes before slicing thinly against the grain.
- Grill vegetables in oil in skillet or on foil on grill.
- Wrap tortillas in foil and warm at the side of the grill or fire.
- Assemble beef, peppers, and onion in tortilla and top as desired.

GRILLED INDIVIDUAL MEAT LOAVES

1 ½ pounds lean ground beef

3/4 -1 cup uncooked, plain oatmeal

1-2 eggs

1 small onion, minced

1 envelope dry vegetable soup mix

- Using your hands, combine all in a bowl or pan and shape into 6 miniature meatloaves.
- Grill, covered, medium-low to medium heat, about 20 minutes.

ANOTHER IDEA: Once cooked, top with slice of cheese, cover grill, and let melt.

Pork *Pork is another meat which lends itself well to the grill: Chops, ham steaks, pork tenderloin….yumm!! The marinades and glazes printed here for pork chops work equally well with pork tenderloin.*

Pork Chops: ½ inch thick chop = one serving

BASIC CHOPS

- Combine all marinade ingredients in one quart, zipper-style plastic bag. Press out air, seal, and massage bag to mix all.
- Reserve some for basting.
- Add chops and marinate 4-6 hours.
- Grill, covered, medium-high heat, turning and basting once for a total of about 8 minutes. Chops can also be fried in a covered skillet instead of grilled.

ASIAN FLAVORED MARINATED GRILLED CHOPS

¼ cup soy sauce

2 teaspoons lime juice

2 teaspoons vegetable oil

1 teaspoon pepper

4 cloves garlic, minced, or 2 teaspoons if from a jar

CHILI BASTED GRILLED CHOPS *Southwestern flavors*

1 cup mayonnaise or salad dressing blend

2 tablespoons lime juice

2 tablespoons cilantro, minced

2 cloves garlic, minced or 1 teaspoon if from a jar

1 teaspoon chili powder or chipotle chili powder

- Blend all and reserve about ½ to pass when serving.
- Grill, covered, medium heat, turning and basting for a total of about 8-10 minutes.
- Serve with reserved chili mayo.

LEMON BASTED GRILLED CHOPS *I sure do love these!*

juice of one lemon

½ stick butter

2 tablespoons bourbon or whiskey

1 tablespoon minced onion or 1 teaspoon onion powder

½ teaspoon bottled hot sauce

a few shakes of salt and pepper

- Combine in small pan, bring to boil, and simmer 3-5 minutes.
- Reserve about ½ to pass when serving.
- Grill, covered, medium heat, turning and basting for a total of about 8-10 minutes.
- Serve with reserved butter sauce.

GARLICKY MARINATED GRILLED CHOPS

½ cup olive oil or vegetable oil

¼ cup chopped parsley

2 tablespoons most any kind of vinegar except fruity ones

4 cloves garlic, minced, or 2 teaspoons if from a jar

JAM GLAZED GRILLED CHOPS

1/3 cup apricot jam or preserves or marmalade

2 tablespoons Dijon mustard

sliced green onions

- Heat in small pan or foil pouch until melted together.
- Grill chops 4-5 minutes, turn and baste with glaze.
- Grill another 4-5 minutes, top with chopped green onions, and serve.

ANOTHER IDEA: Substitute peach jam and add a pinch of red pepper flakes.

SKILLET APPLE CIDER CHOPS *Good with old-fashioned mashed potatoes.*

½ cup apple cider or apple juice

2 tablespoons melted butter

2 green onions, sliced thinly

1 tablespoon chopped parsley

couple dashes salt and pepper

- Place chops in skillet and top with green onions, parsley, salt, and pepper.
- Drizzle with melted butter, cover, and cook 20-25 minutes.
- Remove cover, add apple cider, and cook uncovered 10-15 minutes.

Ham Steaks
Also known as "center cut ham slices," these are generally about one pound, ¼-½ inch thick, and vacuum-packaged. One steak can make 3-4 servings.

BLACKENED HAM STEAK

1-2 tablespoons blackening spice. See recipe in Chapter 1 "Grilled Blackened Chicken Wings."

- Pre-heat grill or skillet to medium hot.
- Rub seasoning on both sides of ham slice.
- Grill or fry, medium-high heat, about 3-4 minutes or until edges start to curl. Flip and cook another 3-4 minutes.

GRILLED HAM AND APPLES

4 apples, cored and sliced ½ inch thick
½ cup orange or peach marmalade
1 tablespoon butter
3-4 dashes ground ginger

- Make basting sauce: Combine jam, butter, and ginger in small pan or foil pouch and cook until melted.
- Start apples on the grill about 6-8 minutes before starting the ham slice.
- Grill apples on a piece of foil on the grate, covered, medium heat for a total of about 15 minutes, turning 3-4 times, basting each time.
- Grill ham slice on the grate, turning once and basting, for a total of about 6-8 minutes.

ANOTHER IDEA: Marmalade and ginger as above, ½ teaspoon dry mustard, 1½ teaspoons lemon juice.

SKILLET PEACHES AND HAM

1—16 ounce can sliced peaches, drained and ½ cup syrup/juice reserved

¼ cup sliced green onions

2 tablespoons brown sugar

2 tablespoons Dijon mustard

- Combine in skillet and heat over medium heat: Syrup, sugar, and mustard.
- Add ham slice and cook 2-3 minutes.
- Turn, add peaches and green onions, and cook another 2-3 minutes.

Pork Tenderloin *All meat, no waste. These are available already flavor injected or plain. A tenderloin takes about 15-18 minutes total grilling time, about 4-5 minutes per side, medium-medium high heat. Let rest 4-5 minutes before slicing.*

SHIRLEY'S MARINADE *My niece Kari's mother-in-law Shirley offers this one.*

¼ cup apricot marmalade

¼ cup teriyaki sauce

½ -1 teaspoon ground ginger

2 cloves garlic, minced, or 1 teaspoon if from a jar

- Combine all in small pan or foil pouch and warm until combined. Reserve a bit for basting.
- Pour remaining marinade in one gallon, zipper-style plastic bag, add tenderloin, squeeze out air, seal, and marinate 1-4 hours.
- Grill, turning 3 times to expose all 4 sides to heat source and basting.

ANOTHER IDEA: Ginger and garlic as above, replace marmalade with soy sauce, replace teriyaki sauce with orange juice, and add a tablespoon of brown sugar.

LEMONY MARINADE

¼ cup lemon juice

2 tablespoons soy sauce

2 cloves garlic, minced or 1 teaspoon if from a jar

- Combine, marinate, and grill as above.

TEXMEX

¼ cup honey

juice of one lime

2 tablespoons chili powder

- Combine, marinate, and grill as above.

ITALIAN DRESSING *The simplest of all!*

½ -1 bottle commercial Italian salad dressing, regular or lite

- Marinate and grill as above.

BROWN SUGAR RUB WITH A BIT OF A BITE

3 tablepoons brown sugar

1½ teaspoons salt

½-1 teaspoon cayenne

- Combine, rub over all sides of tenderloin, and grill as above.

GRILLED PORK TENDERLOIN WITH CREAM SAUCE *Fancy, easy, oh so delicious!*

3 ounces cream cheese or Neufchatel (1/3 less fat), cubed
1/3 cup milk
2 tablespoons chopped chives or green onion tops
2 cloves garlic, minced or 1 teaspoon if from a jar
1 tablespoon butter
salt and pepper: Mix 2 teaspoons salt with 1 teaspoon pepper

- Lightly rub tenderloin with salt and pepper blend.
- Grill as above and start sauce while tenderloin is grilling.
- Melt butter in small pan and sauté the garlic one minute on medium.
- Reduce heat to low and stir in cream cheese cubes, milk, and chives or green onion tops.
- Cook, low, stirring until combined and heated through.
- Serve over pork.

Chicken
Chicken is versatile, equally good as an entrée, sliced into a salad, or served up in a wrap or other sandwich. And boneless, skinless, frozen chicken breasts offer the convenience of going onto the grill without being thawed! If cooking chicken plain, no rub or sauce, you might want to baste with melted butter or oil to preserve moistness.

Sauces for Plain Grilled Chicken

DILL SAUCE *Serve chilled.*

1 cup sour cream or lite sour cream
1 tablespoon lemon juice
1 tablespoon dried dill weed
¼ teaspoon pepper
dash salt

PEACH SAUCE *Warm in small pan or foil pouch.*

1—10 ounce jar peach preserves, jam, or marmalade
3 tablespoons Dijon mustard
2 teaspoons soy sauce

HONEY PECAN SAUCE *Warm in small pan or foil pouch.*

3 tablespoons honey
2 tablespoons butter
2 tablespoons pecan pieces
2 teaspoons lemon juice

CHUNKY PINEAPPLE SAUCE *Warm in small pan or foil pouch.*

1—8 ounce can pineapple tidbits, drained

1 tablespoon honey

1 scant tablespoon butter

> TIP: Dry rubs can be patted onto the individual chicken pieces or placed in a clean plastic or paper bag, chicken pieces added, and shaken to coat.

MEDIUM SPICY PAPRIKA RUB

¼ cup paprika

1 tablespoon salt or kosher salt

¼ - ½ teaspoon pepper

ANOTHER IDEA: Add some heat! Jazz it up by adding ½-1 teaspoon cayenne.

CHILI DRY RUB *Makes enough for 2-3 cook-outs. Store extra in a tightly closed container.*

¼ cup chili powder

1 tablespoon onion powder

1 tablespoon ground cumin

2 teaspoon salt

1 teaspoon dried oregano

1 teaspoon garlic powder

1 teaspoon cayenne

BASIC MARINATED GRILLED CHICKEN

- Assemble all but chicken in gallon sized, zipper-style plastic bag, squeeze out air, seal, and massage bag to combine all.
- Reserve some for basting.
- Add chicken pieces: Breasts, wings, drumsticks, whatever, and marinate ½ to one hour.
- Grill, medium, turning and basting frequently, total of 15-35 minutes depending on the thickness of the chicken pieces.

ASIAN MARINADE *Good on pork, too.*

1/3 cup orange juice

1/3 cup soy sauce

2 tablespoons chopped parsley

2 tablespoons vegetable oil

1 clove garlic, minced or ½ teaspoon if from a jar

LIME MARINADE

3 tablespoons lime juice

2 tablespoons olive oil

1 teaspoon salt

½ teaspoon pepper

ANOTHER IDEA: Add 2 tablespoons honey, 1 teaspoon steak seasoning, and 1 teaspoon ground cumin.

TEQUILA-LIME MARINADE

1 fresh lime: If squeezed will give you ¼ cup lime juice and provide for 2 teaspoons grated (or finely minced) lime peel/zest (just the green part) or ¼ cup bottled lime juice and forget the peel

¼ cup vegetable oil

2 tablespoons chopped cilantro or parsley

2-3 teaspoons tequila

½ teaspoon sugar

½ teaspoon salt

1 clove garlic, minced or ½ teaspoon if from a jar

1 jalapeno, seeded and diced

LEMONADE AND RUM MARINADE *My daughter's father-in-law Jeff grilled drumsticks marinated in this one very hot and humid August day at their lake home in North Webster, Indiana. Being splashed with cooling waves on the pontoon boat ride after lunch felt wonderful!*

1—6 ounce can frozen lemonade concentrate, thawed but not diluted

½ cup soy sauce

¼ cup rum

2 teaspoons seasoned salt

1 teaspoon celery salt

½ teaspoon garlic powder

couple dashes bottled hot sauce

TERIYAKI PINEAPPLE MARINADE

1—8 ounce can crushed pineapple, drained

¼ cup teriyaki sauce

2 tablespoons lemon juice

2 tablespoons red wine vinegar

1 tablespoon olive oil or vegetable oil

2 cloves garlic, minced, or 1 teaspoon if from a bottle

CAJUN MARINADE *Not too spicy; add more cayenne to add heat.*

¼ cup soy sauce

1 tablespoon bottled hot sauce

1 tablespoon onion powder

1 teaspoon thyme

½ teaspoon cayenne

CALIFORNIA MARINADE

2 tablespoons cider vinegar

2 tablespoons olive oil

1 tablespoon Dijon mustard

½ teaspoon dried dill weed

½ teaspoon pepper

½ teaspoon onion salt or onion powder and a few dashes of salt

SOUTHWESTERN MARINADE

½ cup beer

1 tablespoon chopped cilantro

1 tablespoon soy sauce

2 teaspoons minced jalapeno (no seeds) or pickled jalapeno

2 teaspoons lime juice

salt and pepper

BOURBON MARINADE

1/3 cup bourbon

3 tablespoons packed brown sugar

2 tablespoons soy sauce

1 ½ tablespoons lemon juice

1 tablespoon olive oil

1 clove garlic, minced or ½ teaspoon if from a jar

Glazes
Be careful with sweet glazes as the sugar in them will burn quickly. Glaze only after turning the final time so the glaze is never directly exposed to the heat source. Warm glaze ingredients in a small pan or foil pouch.

SWEET AND SOUR APRICOT GLAZED GRILLED CHICKEN

2/3 cup apricot preserves, jam, or marmalade

¼ cup white wine vinegar

2 tablespoons hot mustard

2 cloves garlic minced or 1 teaspoon if from a jar

ORANGE AND HONEY GLAZED GRILLED CHICKEN

¼ cup honey

¼ cup orange marmalade

½ teaspoon ground ginger

ANOTHER IDEA: Reserve some of the glaze. Drain 1—11 ounce can mandarin oranges and 1—8 ounce can pineapple tidbits. Warm fruit in small pan or foil pouch. Top grilled chicken with warm fruit and drizzle with reserved glaze.

Lamb
Lamb offers a tasty alternative to the usual grilled meats. Lamb chops are my favorite, marinated 20-30 minutes, and then grilled. Figure on two chops per person. Grill 5-6 minutes per side, medium hot, or 7-8 minutes on medium, or fry in skillet.

ROSEMARY LEMON MARINADE

¼ cup lemon juice

1 tablespoon olive oil

2 cloves garlic minced or 1 teaspoon if from a jar

fresh rosemary twig or 1 teaspoon crushed rosemary

OREGANO LEMON MARINADE

1/3 cup olive oil

3 tablespoons lemon juice

2 tablespoons red wine vinegar

1 tablespoon chopped fresh oregano or 1 teaspoon dried oregano

WET RUB

2 tablespoons olive oil

1 tablespoon minced garlic

1 tablespoon fresh rosemary or 1 teaspoon dried rosemary

½ teaspoon salt

¼ teaspoon red pepper flakes

- Mix all together and press onto both sides of chops.

Fish

I was raised in the cornfields of southern Minnesota a long time ago, and seafood was just not a family menu item. Oh, sure, you could order deep-fried shrimp at the drive-in, but that was about the extent of it, except for pan fish we caught in the lakes. Imagine my delight later in life learning about such things as tilapia, scallops, salmon, crab, and grilled fresh shrimp, not deep-fried! Like a kid in a candy store!

BASIC FISH *Fish can be cooked in foil and steamed, fried in oil in a skillet, or simply grilled. Always cook fish until it flakes easily when pierced with a fork. If you take it off the heat before this, it will just be rubbery and unfit to eat, so be patient! Flavored crumb breading, spices, and sauces on the side add spark to the flesh and will keep you coming back for more!*

STEAMED FISH *Place fish on a double sheet of foil with enough to fold over and encase it with some air room. Season as desired, sprinkle with lemon juice, and seal up the packet. Steam on grill or over grate of a wood fire.*

FRIED FISH *The fish can be battered or not, fried in oil or butter, turned just once. Nothing is better than fresh-caught walleye fried simply in butter and sprinkled with garlic salt! (Especially if you caught these beauties out on the lake before dawn and are now enjoying with fried eggs for breakfast---yes, there is a happy memory in that picture! Thanks Fred, Russ, and Doris.)*

GRILLED FISH *Fish can be placed directly on the grill surface or on a piece of aluminum foil. When the fish is ready to turn, it will separate easily from the grill. If it sticks, it's not ready yet, so give it another minute and try again.*

Salmon

My personal opinion is that the best salmon is the first run in early spring from the just opened, ice cold rivers in Alaska! Grill on foil on medium with lid closed and not turning the fish. Grill until fish flakes easily and separates easily from the skin. Leave the skin on the foil and throw foil and skin away.

GRILLED BROWN SUGAR SALMON *The sugar will burn if it gets on the coals, so put a slightly larger second sheet of foil with the edges rolled up to form a "pan" under the sheet you are cooking the fish on to catch those sugar drips. It will still burn, but is easy clean-up!*

- Sprinkle brown sugar liberally over a piece of salmon on foil and grill with a closed grill lid.
- Remove when the flesh flakes easily (about 10 minutes if thin piece) and separates from the skin. Throw skin and foil away.

SOY SAUCE AND DIJON GARLIC MARINATED STEAMED SALMON

1 cup soy sauce

¼ cup Dijon mustard

2 cloves garlic minced or 1 teaspoon if from a jar

- Marinate salmon in one gallon, plastic storage bag in the cooler for 1 hour.
- Remove from marinade and place on large sheet of heavy duty foil.
- Tope with a second sheet of foil and fold edges together to seal.
- Cook on medium grill until salmon flakes easily, 15-20 minutes, depending on thickness of salmon.
- Serve with "Pineapple and Red Pepper Salsa" from Chapter 1 Appetizers.

EASY GRILLED SALMON

- Top a piece of salmon on foil with mayonnaise or sour cream or ranch dressing or olive oil and kosher salt, and sprinkle liberally with dill weed.
- Remove when the flesh flakes easily (about 10 minutes if thin piece) and separates from the skin. Throw skin and foil away.
- Serve with yogurt cucumber sauce. See recipe in this chapter.

WINE AND LEMON MARINATED GRILLED SALMON

1/3 cup dry white wine

1/3 cup olive oil

1 tablespoon lemon juice

2 cloves garlic minced or 1 teaspoon if from a jar

½ teaspoon salt

3-4 dashes pepper

minced parsley

- Reserve some of the marinade for basting.
- Marinate one hour in cooler in sealed one gallon, zipper-style plastic bag.
- Grill directly on grate without placing on foil, medium heat, 4-5 minutes and then turn.
- Grill second side another 4-5 minutes, basting with the marinade.

GRILLED SALMON BASTED WITH HERBED BUTTER

¼ cup butter

1 green onion and tops, sliced

1 tablespoon chopped fresh chives or freeze-dried chives or 1 teaspoon dried

1 tablespoon fresh tarragon or 1 teaspoon dried

1½ tablespoon chopped parsley

1 tablespoon Dijon mustard

couple dashes pepper

- Combine in small pan or foil pouch until butter melts and use to baste salmon as it grills.
- Place salmon on foil before placing on grill—butter leaking down on the heat source will burn and cause smoking.

Catfish

GRILLED CATFISH

1/3 cup lime juice

¼ cup olive oil

1/8 teaspoon salt

- Combine in one gallon, zipper-style plastic bag, add catfish fillets or nuggets, and marinate 15-30 minutes.
- Spray foil and place fish on foil.
- Cover grill and cook 7-8 minutes per side, turning once.

SPICY BLACKENED GRILLED CATFISH

2-3 tablespoons lemon juice in a flat pan or on a plate

1 teaspoon lemon pepper

1 teaspoon pepper

1 teaspoon Cajun or Creole seasoning

1 teaspoon blackening spice mix. See "Blackened Burgers."

- Pre-heat grill to medium.
- Combine spices.
- Dip catfish pieces in lemon juice, coat lightly with spices, and place on grill or in skillet.
- Grill, covered, medium heat, turning once, about 8 minutes per side or until fish flakes easily.
- Serve with tartar sauce. See recipe in this chapter.

ANOTHER IDEA: Add minced jalapeno peppers to the tartar sauce.

Tilapia

ASIAN-FLAVORED MARINATED GRILLED FISH

fish of choice: Mine is tilapia but you could certainly use some other variety

1/3 cup vegetable oil

¼ cup soy sauce

¼ cup lemon juice

1 teaspoon garlic salt

2 cloves garlic minced or 1 teaspoon if from a jar

½ teaspoon ground ginger

- Place all but fish in one gallon, zipper-style plastic bag, squeeze out air, seal, and massage bag to combine all.
- Reserve some for basting.
- Add fish and marinate, chilled, 10 minutes. It doesn't take long since fish is such a delicate flesh.
- Grill low heat, basting, and turning once for a total of about 15 minutes.

GRILLED FISH TACOS

fish of choice; again, I lean toward tilapia

1 tablespoon lime juice

2 teaspoons ground cumin

taco shells

salsa

shredded lettuce

shredded cheese: Mexi-blend, taco, Monterey jack, Cheddar

diced tomato

sour cream or lite sour cream

- Sprinkle fish with lime juice and cumin.
- Grill or steam as you like until fish flakes easily.
- Break fish into pieces and assemble tacos with fish pieces and toppings of your choice.

Fish Seasoning, Basting Butter, and Sauces

HOMEMADE SEAFOOD SEASONING

¼ cup dried parsley

3 tablespoons dried dill weed

3 tablespoons lemon pepper

½ teaspoon ground bay leaves or 4 bay leaves, finely crumbled

- Mix and store in a tightly sealed container.

CHIVE BUTTER FOR BASTING FISH, SHRIMP, OR SCALLOPS

1 stick butter, melted

3 tablespoons chopped fresh chives

2 tablespoons Dijon mustard

2 tablespoons lemon juice

- Reserve some for serving time.

BASIC TARTAR SAUCE *This is also good on a wrap sandwich.*

1 cup mayonnaise or sour cream or lite sour cream

2 tablespoons lemon juice

2 tablespoons chopped dill pickle or dill pickle relish squeezed dry (Squeeze it in your hand and just let the juice drip onto the ground---you are outside, right?)

1 tablespoon minced onion

1 teaspoon Worcestershire sauce

HORSERADISH TARTAR SAUCE

1 cup mayonnaise or salad dressing blend

¼ cup chopped sweet pickles or sweet pickle relish squeezed dry

1 tablespoon lemon juice

1 tablespoon prepared horseradish

SPICY MAYO SAUCE *This one has some bite to it!*

1 cup mayonnaise or salad dressing blend

2 tablespoons lemon juice

½ teaspoon salt

1/8 teaspoon cayenne—or more if you like things hot!

dash or 2 bottled hot sauce

CUCUMBER YOGURT SAUCE FOR GRILLED SALMON *My favorite!*

¾ cup plain yogurt

½ cup peeled, seeded, and diced cucumber

¼ cup mayonnaise

1 tablespoon minced onion

1 teaspoon chopped parsley

¼ teaspoon dried dill weed

1/8 teaspoon salt

SEAFOOD REMOULADE *Just a fancy French word for a mayo sauce to accompany chicken, fish, or other seafood. Used in the South, it means "spicy" and this one doesn't disappoint!*

1/3 cup mayonnaise or salad dressing blend
1/3 cup minced parsley
2 tablespoons prepared horseradish
2 tablespoons Creole mustard
2 tablespoons Dijon mustard
1 tablespoon lemon juice
1 bunch green onions and tops, sliced

- Combine all and chill.

Shrimp *The size to buy depends on the method of preparation, the dish you are making, and your budget. You can buy them peeled and deveined for just a bit more, or you can do the work yourself. On larger shrimp it is very important that they be deveined or the flavor will be impaired. Heads and tails can be left on.*

If cooking on skewers, either use a flat metal skewer so the shrimp can't twist or use two round skewers so that once on the skewer, the skewers look like train tracks through the shrimp, preventing them from twisting. Wooden skewers must be soaked thoroughly about 20 minutes before using so they won't catch fire on the grill.

To keep the bare ends of the skewers from flaming while cooking, place a couple layers of aluminum foil on the edge of the grill to lay the bare ends of the skewers on. Protect your fingers with a kitchen towel or potholder when retrieving hot skewers.

GARLIC GRILLED SHRIMP

1 pound large shrimp, peeled and deveined

¾ cup butter

10 cloves garlic, minced, or 5 teaspoons if from a jar

2 tablespoons lemon juice

¼ teaspoon cayenne

- In skillet or medium-sized pan melt butter and sauté garlic one minute.
- Add lemon juice and cayenne, bring to boil, and cook one minute.
- Add shrimp, remove from heat, and let sit for 20 minutes in a cooler or on ice.
- Assemble on skewers, leaving a little air space between each shrimp for even cooking.
- Grill, medium hot, 4 minutes per side.

CHILI GRILLED SHRIMP

1 pound large shrimp, peeled and deveined

¼ cup packed brown sugar

2 tablespoons olive oil or vegetable oil

2 tablespoons chili powder

1 tablespoon garlic powder

1 teaspoon salt or kosher salt

- Combine all but shrimp in one gallon, zipper-style plastic bag, squeeze out air, seal, and massage bag to combine.
- Add shrimp, seal, and massage bag again.
- Thread onto skewers and grill, medium hot, 4 minutes per side.

CREOLE GRILLED SHRIMP

1 pound large shrimp, peeled and deveined

1 tablespoon olive oil

2 teaspoons Creole seasoning

- Assemble on skewers, leaving a little air space between each shrimp for even cooking.
- Combine olive oil and seasoning and baste shrimp as they cook.
- Grill, basting, medium hot, 4 minutes per side.

SASSY GRILLED SHRIMP *These are fabulous!! Son-in-law Mike made them for my birthday last summer. Thank you, my dear!*

large or jumbo shrimp, deveined but not peeled

3 tablespoons olive oil

2 teaspoons paprika

salt and pepper

1/3 cup minced parsley

½ stick butter, melted

3 tablespoons lemon juice

2 tablespoons bottled hot sauce

1 tablespoon minced garlic or 3 teaspoons if from a jar

4 dashes Worcestershire sauce

lemon wedges

- Combine parsley, butter, lemon juice, hot sauce, garlic, and Worcestershire in one gallon, plastic storage bag and set aside. NOTE: You'll be tossing the grilled shrimp in this mixture when taking it off the grill, so keep this at the ready when putting shrimp on the grill.
- Combine olive oil, paprika, salt and pepper and coat raw shrimp in a bowl, using clean fingers to toss.
- Assemble on skewers, leaving a little air space between each shrimp for even cooking.
- Grill, medium hot, 4 minutes per side.
- Slip off skewers into prepared and waiting bag of butter and spices and toss.
- Serve with lemon wedges and a paper towel for removing shells. Have a plate or bucket on the picnic table for tossing the shells.

TEQUILA LIME GRILLED SHRIMP

1 pound large shrimp, peeled and deveined

¼ cup olive oil

2 tablespoons tequila

2 tablespoons lime juice

1 green onion + green top, sliced

1 clove garlic minced or ½ teaspoons if from a jar

1 teaspoon ground cumin

1 teaspoon salt

- Combine all but shrimp in one gallon, zipper-style plastic bag, squeeze out air, seal, and massage bag to combine.
- Add shrimp, seal, massage bag again, and marinate in cooler one hour.
- Thread onto skewers and grill, medium hot, 4 minutes per side.

Skewers

"Dinner on a stick!" When cooking on skewers, either use a flat metal skewer so the ingredients can't twist or use two round skewers so that once on the skewer, the skewers look like train tracks through the skewered items, thus preventing them from twisting. Wooden skewers must be soaked thoroughly about 20 minutes before using so they won't catch fire on the grill.

TIP: *If you happen to have an empty wine bottle or 2 liter pop bottle, fill it with water and soak skewers in it.*

Different densities call for differing cooking times, so you may want to do the meat and the different vegetables on separate skewers. For example, cherry tomatoes only have to get hot, about 4-5 minutes, while green pepper pieces take 15 minutes to cook. Rather than having each person make his own meal on one skewer, you could cook all the meat on one skewer, all the potatoes on another, all the fruits on a third skewer, and so on.

Place a couple layers of aluminum foil on the edge of the grill to lay the bare end of wooden skewers on to keep them from flaming while cooking. They'll be hot when removed from grill, so protect your hand.

INGREDIENT GRILLING MINUTES

Chicken	15-20
Ham	5-7
Lamb	10-12
Scallops	7-10
Shrimp	4-5
Sirloin	15-20

Cherry tomatoes	5
Mushrooms	5
Onion	15-20
Peach	5-7
Peppers	10-15
Pineapple	5-7
Potatoes parboiled: Cook in boiling water 7-8 minutes to soften	15

Beef *Usually sirloin cut into 1 – 1½ inch cubes/chunks plus veggies and/or fruit of choice. Reserve some marinade to use to baste kabobs while grilling, and marinate beef in remaining marinade 1 hour or so before assembling skewers.*

BASIC BEEF KABOBS

1 pound sirloin, cubed

½ cup vegetable oil or olive oil

¼ cup red wine

2 cloves garlic, minced, or 1 teaspoon if from a jar

½ teaspoon salt

- Marinate steak in above ingredients for one hour in a one gallon, zipper-style plastic storage bag in cooler.
- Have each diner assemble his own "meal on a stick": Cherry tomatoes, red and green pepper chunks, onion wedges, pre-cooked small potatoes, fresh mushrooms, pineapple wedges, peach halves, whatever! Or assemble single ingredient skewers for the separate ingredients.
- Cook over fire, turning and basting.

TANGY MARINADE *Low fat, low cal.*

3 tablespoons red wine vinegar

2 tablespoons Worcestershire

3-4 garlic cloves, minced, or 2 teaspoons if from a jar

SHERRY MARINADE

¼ cup sherry

1½ tablespoons soy sauce

1 tablespoon red wine vinegar

1 tablespoon ketchup

1 tablespoon honey

2 garlic cloves minced or 1 teaspoon if from a jar

WHISKEY MARINADE

¼ cup whiskey

¼ cup soy sauce

2 tablespoons vegetable oil

2 tablespoons lemon juice

½ teaspoon pepper

LEMON BUTTER BASTING SAUCE *Try this instead of a marinade.*

1 stick butter

¼ cup lemon juice

3 tablespoons chopped fresh or freeze dried chives or green onion tops

1 tablespoon Worcestershire sauce

1 teaspoon prepared mustard

½ teaspoon salt

- Heat all in small pan or foil pouch. Reserve 1/3 cup to pass at serving time.

HAM AND FRESH PEACH KABOBS *This makes both a pretty and pretty quick meal!*

1 center cut ham steak, sliced into 1-1½ inch chunks

1 fresh peach per diner

green pepper chunks

¼ cup orange marmalade

2 tablespoon vegetable oil

1 tablespoon Dijon mustard

1 tablespoon lemon juice

- Make basting sauce: Combine jam, oil, mustard, and lemon juice in small pan or foil pouch and warm to combine all.
- Peel peaches if desired, split, remove pit, and cut each half in two to make 4 pieces per kabob.
- Assemble kabobs and grill 6-8 minutes, turning and basting 2-3 times.

Chicken *Boneless, skinless chicken breast or thigh cut into strips or chunks, marinated ½-1 hour. Reserve some marinade for basting before adding chicken to the bag.*

BASIC MARINADE

¼ cup soy sauce

¼ cup bottled Italian salad dressing

2 teaspoons lemon juice

1 clove garlic minced or ½ teaspoon if from a jar

ASIAN-FLAVORED MARINADE

1—15.25 ounce can pineapple chunks, drained and 1/3 cup syrup/juice reserved

½ cup soy sauce

1/3 cup sugar

2 cloves garlic minced or 1 teaspoon if from a jar

½ teaspoon ground ginger

- Suggested kabob: Chicken, pineapple chunk, green pepper chunk. Repeat.

ORANGE JUICE MARINADE

1/3 cup orange juice

¼ cup white or blush wine

2 tablespoons olive oil

2 tablespoons Worcestershire sauce

½ teaspoon ground ginger

1 garlic clove minced or ½ teaspoon if from a jar

Lamb *Lamb is the original "shish kebab" and takes about 10-12 minutes total grilling time.*

1 pound boneless lamb, cut into 1-1½ inch cubes

¼ cup soy sauce

¼ cup vinegar

¼ cup vegetable oil

2 cloves garlic minced or 1 teaspoon if from a jar

¼ teaspoon ground ginger (optional)

Seafood *Think large shrimp, peeled and deveined, and sea scallops---yum!*

SHRIMP + PINEAPPLE KABOBS

1 pound large shrimp

1—8 ounce can pineapple chunks, drained and juice/syrup reserved

¼ cup ballpark mustard

- Combine juice and mustard in one gallon, zipper-style plastic bag. Reserve some for basting before adding shrimp.
- Marinate shrimp in juice and mustard for ½-1 hour, chilled.
- Grill, medium high, 3-4 minutes per side, basting and turning.

SCALLOPS + PINEAPPLE KABOBS

1 pound sea scallops. Remove "foot" if present.

1—15 ounce can pineapple chunks, drained and juice/syrup reserved

¼ cup white wine

¼ cup soy sauce

2 tablespoons lemon juice

2 tablespoons minced fresh parsley

2 cloves garlic, minced, or 1 teaspoon if from a jar

pepper

- Combine all in one gallon, zipper-style plastic storage bag, squeeze out air, seal, and massage bag to combine. Reserve some for basting.
- Add scallops, squeeze out air, seal, and marinate 1 hour, chilled.
- Assemble kabobs and grill a total of 10-12 minutes on high, turning and basting.

SHRIMP AND SCALLOP KABOBS *This is a seafood treat!*

3 large shrimp, peeled and deveined, per person

2-3 sea scallops per person. Remove "foot" if present.

½ cup vegetable oil or olive oil

¼ cup lime juice

1 tablespoon minced onion

2 cloves garlic minced or 1 teaspoon if from a jar

¼ teaspoon salt

¼ teaspoon pepper

- Marinate an hour, chilled, and then grill on skewers, medium-high heat, 7-8 minutes per side.

VEGETABLES and SIDE DISHES

Potatoes *Meat and potatoes go together like bacon and eggs!*

BASIC STEAMED POTATOES
Instead of boiling potatoes in a pan, grill in foil.

4-5 new red potatoes or small "B" sized red potatoes per person, scrubbed and left whole if really small or cut in half or quarters to make a bit larger than bite-sized pieces. No need to peel.

2-3 tablespoons butter

chopped onion or chives (optional)

salt and pepper

- Place potatoes and chopped onion or chives on a double thickness of aluminum foil with enough extra foil to make a packet with a bit of air space.
- Dot with butter and add salt and pepper before sealing packet.
- Place on medium-low to medium heat and cook 20-25 minutes until potatoes are easily pierced. Rotate a couple times.
- Serve out of foil pack with extra butter if desired.

ANOTHER IDEA: Any leftover potatoes are tasty when fried for breakfast. Consider cooking extra---then they are "planned overs" not leftovers! —so you have enough for a breakfast.

ANOTHER IDEA: Dress with this homemade dressing before serving---tasty! Reminds me of old-fashioned German potato salad without the bacon.

¼ cup vegetable oil

2 tablespoons tarragon vinegar (or substitute white wine vinegar)

1 clove garlic minced or ½ teaspoon if from a jar

¾ teaspoon Worcestershire sauce

¾ teaspoon seasoned salt

1-2 dashes of sugar

- Shake vigorously in a tightly covered container.

BBQ POTATOES IN FOIL

½ large baking potato per person, peeled if you want to, and sliced into ¼-½ inch slices

2-3 tablespoons butter

1 tablespoon honey

2 teaspoons chili powder

1 garlic clove minced or ½ teaspoon if from a jar

salt and pepper

- Prepare and serve as for "Steamed Potatoes" above.

CHEESY POTATOES IN FOIL *Minimal prep, maximum flavor! I recommend spraying the foil with non-stick spray as the cheese tends to stick to the foil otherwise.*

4 cups frozen hash browns, thawed or not

1 cup shredded Cheddar cheese

½ cup commercial ranch dressing

grated Parmesan cheese

- Prepare and serve as for "Steamed Potatoes" above except check to see if the potatoes are done by sampling a forkful from the middle of the packet.
- Garnish with Parmesan.

PARTY POTATOES IN FOIL

1 pound package frozen hash browns, thawed or not

1—10.25 ounce can cream of mushroom or cream of celery soup

1 cup shredded Cheddar cheese

½ stick butter

½ cup sour cream or lite sour cream

sliced green onions and tops

- Prepare as for "Steamed Potatoes" above except check to see if the potatoes are done by sampling a forkful from the middle of the packet.

MUSHROOM SWISS POTATOES IN FOIL *A little more work, but so good!*

6 russet potatoes, peeled and diced into ½ inch (bite-sized) cubes

1 tablespoon vegetable oil or 2-3 tablespoons butter

½ pound fresh mushrooms, sliced

1 teaspoon vegetable oil

TOPPINGS

4 ounces shredded Swiss cheese

¼ cup sour cream or lite sour cream

¼ cup chopped parsley (optional)

4-6 slices crisply cooked, crumbled bacon

- Cook potatoes and butter or oil as for "Steamed Potatoes" above.
- Place mushrooms and oil in foil pack as you did for the potatoes, and start on the grill about 10 minutes before the potatoes are due to be done.
- While potatoes and mushrooms cook: Fry bacon and crumble.
- When potatoes are done, add the cheese and seal loosely so the cheese melts.
- Pass the sour cream, parsley, and bacon so diners can top their potatoes as they want.

GRILL ROASTED POTATOES *A "grill topper" is helpful when grilling potato pieces to keep potatoes from being lost into the grill or fire. A sheet of foil on the grill works, too. These are roasted on the grill, not placed into a foil packet.*

4-5 new red potatoes or small "B" sized red potatoes per person, scrubbed and cut in half but not peeled or

½ baking potato per person cut into ½ inch slices, peeled or not as you wish

2 tablespoons vegetable or olive oil

salt and pepper or seasoning salt

- Toss potatoes in oil and season as desired.
- Grill, medium-high, turning once or twice, 10-15 minutes.

GRILLED STEAK FRIES

1 pound bag frozen steak fries, thawed or 3 baking potatoes cut into wedges

¼ cup vegetable or olive oil

1 teaspoon garlic salt

1 teaspoon seasoned salt

½ teaspoon paprika

- Place all in a one gallon, zipper-style plastic bag, squeeze out air, seal, and massage bag.
- Grill, medium-high, turning once or twice, 10-15 minutes.

ANOTHER IDEA: Use a southwestern seasoning mix by additionally adding to the bag:

1 teaspoon cumin

½ teaspoon paprika

¼ teaspoon cayenne

MARINATED GRILLED POTATOES

potatoes, peeled or not as you wish, cut into wedges or planks as you like

½-1 bottle commercial Italian salad dressing; reserve a little for basting

- Place all in a one gallon, zipper-style plastic bag, squeeze out air, seal, and massage bag.
- Grill, medium-high, turning and basting, 10-15 minutes.

SKILLET FRIED POTATOES *You can fry fresh potatoes or boiled potatoes. Fresh take longer to cook.*

1-2 red potatoes per person, peeled or not, already boiled or not, cut into slices

2 tablespoons vegetable oil

- If using fresh potatoes, pat dry before adding to hot oil in skillet.
- Try to layer slices in the pan so they cook evenly.
- Turn only once and ensure you have a nice, crispy crust on the bottom before turning the first time: Lift the edge with your spatula and take a peek.

ANOTHER IDEA: You can jazz these up in so many ways to fit your menu----add chopped onion or peppers or sliced green onions with tops or sliced jalapenos or chopped chives or spices like seasoned salt, red pepper flakes, cumin, or cayenne or top with shredded cheese and let melt.

BASIC SWEET POTATOES IN FOIL *Use either fresh yams or sweet potatoes.*

3-4 yams, peeled and sliced in ¼ inch slices

¼ cup butter

salt and pepper

- Place potatoes on a double thickness of aluminum foil with enough extra foil to make a packet with a bit of air space.
- Dot with butter and add salt and pepper before sealing packet.
- Place on medium-low to medium heat and cook 20-25 minutes until potatoes are easily pierced. Rotate a couple times.
- You can mash these or serve as they are.

ANOTHER IDEA: If mashing, add a bit more butter and a couple tablespoons orange juice if you want.

SWEET POTATOES AND APPLES IN MAPLE SYRUP IN FOIL

packet of sweet potatoes as above in "Basic Sweet Potatoes in Foil"

2 tart apples, cored and cut into wedges or chunks, skin on

¼ cup maple syrup

½ stick butter, divided

2 tablespoons brown sugar

dash cinnamon

- Place potatoes and apples on a double thickness of aluminum foil with enough extra foil to make a packet with a bit of air space.
- Dot with 2 tablespoons butter and add salt and pepper before sealing packet.
- Place on medium-low to medium heat and cook 20-25 minutes until potatoes are easily pierced. Rotate a couple times.
- Melt in small pan or aluminum foil pouch: Maple syrup, 2 tablespoons butter, brown sugar, and cinnamon.
- Pour over cooked potatoes and apples and scoop out some of the syrup onto each plate when serving.

SUPER SMASHED POTATOES AND SWEET POTATOES *Your taste buds will be delighted!*

1 red potato per person + ½ a sweet potato (or yam) per person, peeled and cut into small chunks
½ cup milk
¼ cup butter
¼ cup sour cream or lite sour cream
¼ cup grated Parmesan cheese
1 tablespoon horseradish
salt and pepper to taste
dash or two cinnamon and or nutmeg

- Cook potatoes by either boiling in salted water or cooking on grill or grate in foil, 20-25 minutes until easily pierced with a fork.
- Drain potatoes and mash with all other ingredients. Use a fork to "smash" the potatoes and combine all ingredients using the back of one of your large serving spoons. (Or bring a potato masher along, but I did say no special tools, didn't I??)

Rice

Rice goes with many meals and there are a variety of ways to prepare it. The easiest (and most expensive) way is to purchase the rice sold as "boil in a bag". Consider another "boil in a bag" method: Cook the rice at home, seal in freezer quality, quart-sized plastic bags, and drop into boiling water at the site---so much more economical and really not much more prep. (Plus you'll have a pan of hot water for washing dishes!) Boxed rice mixes are another possibility as these contain the flavoring packets and spices needed for the dish. Or you can simply cook the rice at the site in a heavy pan with a lid.

BASIC WHITE RICE *Make in a large pan with a lid or a covered skillet.*

2 cups liquid

I cup raw white rice, long grain is preferable

I teaspoon salt

- Place all in heavy lidded pan and bring to boil.
- Reduce heat, keep covered, and cook on low 22-25 minutes until rice is done. Test by removing cover and tasting a rice kernel or two.
- Let stand 5 minutes with the cover on.
- Fluff with a fork and serve.
- Immediately fill empty pan with cold water, couple dashes dishwashing detergent, and let soak while you enjoy dinner.

PINEAPPLE RICE *Makes a nice side dish with stir fry or chicken.*

I—8 ounce can pineapple tidbits, drained

chopped parsley for color

- Add pineapple and parsley to cooked rice and allow to warm through.

DIRTY RICE

3 cups chicken broth or water

1 ½ cup raw white rice

½ pound bulk pork sausage

½ cup diced red onion

¼ cup celery, diced

¼ cup red bell pepper, diced

3-4 cloves garlic, minced, or 2 teaspoons if from a jar

1 teaspoon salt

3-5 dashes cayenne

- In skillet sauté sausage in oil for a couple minutes, separating and turning.
- Add veggies and continue to stir and cook another couple minutes.
- Add the raw rice and continue stirring and cooking another couple minutes.
- Add chicken broth or water, salt, and cayenne, cover, and bring to boil.
- Cook as above for "Basic White Rice."

SPANISH RICE

2 cups water

1—14.5 ounce can diced tomatoes, with or without green chiles, with liquid

1 cup raw white rice

1 green pepper, seeded and coarsely chopped

1 onion, chopped

3 tablespoons vegetable oil

1 teaspoon salt

- Sauté onion and pepper in oil in skillet 4-5 minutes.
- Add rice, stir, and cook until golden.
- Add water, tomatoes and liquid, and salt and cook as above for "Basic White Rice."

WILD RICE SIDE DISH

1 cup uncooked wild rice and white rice blend, cooked per package directions

1—6 ounce jar marinated artichoke hearts, drained and chopped a bit if too big

12 cherry tomatoes or grape tomatoes, halved

2/3 cup frozen peas, thawed

¼ cup slivered almonds

3-4 green onions and tops, sliced

1 bottle commercial Italian salad dressing, use as much as you think is needed

- Toss all but almonds and chill.
- Toss again at serving time, adding the almonds and perhaps a bit more dressing.

Asparagus *Asparagus can be boiled, steamed, or grilled and served hot or cold. Length of cooking time depends on thickness of spears. Although sold by the pound, it is marketed in a bundle, so don't be mislead that the price is per bundle. Be savvy! You must snap off the bottoms, leaving only the tender tops to cook.*

STEAM: Make aluminum foil packet using double thickness foil, drizzle lightly with olive oil, and seal. Grill about 8-10 minutes.

BOIL: Place in boiling water and cook about 6-8 minutes. Plunge into an ice bath.

ROAST: Toss with olive oil and place on aluminum foil or grill topper. Grill, turning, about 5-6 minutes.

LEMON DRESSING

1 teaspoon olive oil

½ teaspoon lemon juice

1 clove garlic minced or ½ teaspoon if from a jar

salt and pepper

- Shake vigorously in tightly covered container. Pour over hot, cooked asparagus.

ASPARAGUS AND TOMATOES

1 pound asparagus, grilled as above

2 tomatoes, sliced

1/3 cup vegetable oil or olive oil

¼ cup red wine vinegar

1 tablespoons chopped fresh chives or green onion tops

2 teaspoons dried, crushed oregano

- Place tomato slices on serving dish and top with grilled asparagus.
- Shake vinegar, oil, chives, oregano, salt, and pepper in tightly covered container and pour over.

DILL PICKLE DRESSED ASPARAGUS *This is especially good cold—tastes "pickled."*

1 pound asparagus, cooked by any method above

¼ cup vegetable oil

3 tablespoons cider vinegar

1 tablespoon minced dill pickle or dill pickle relish

salt and pepper to taste

- Shake vinegar, oil, pickle, salt, and pepper in tightly covered container and pour over.

Broccoli

BASIC COOKED BROCCOLI

2 cups fresh broccoli crowns

2 tablespoons water

- Place broccoli on a double thickness of aluminum foil with enough extra foil to make a packet with a bit of air space.
- Add water and seal.
- Place on medium-low to medium heat and cook 10 minutes until done.

BROCCOLI WITH HORSERADISH BUTTER

one recipe basic cooked broccoli

½ cup mayonnaise or salad dressing blend

2 tablespoons butter

1 tablespoon horseradish

1 tablespoon minced onion

salt to taste

- Combine all but cooked broccoli in small pan or aluminum pouch and cook until butter is melted.
- Pour over cooked broccoli.

BROCCOLI AND SUMMER SQUASH GRILL PACKET

½ of 5 ounce can sliced water chestnuts, drained; use the rest in a green salad

2 cups fresh broccoli crowns

1 zucchini, sliced

1 yellow squash, sliced

4-6 green onions, sliced

2 tablespoons butter

- Place all on a double thickness of aluminum foil with enough extra foil to make a packet with a bit of air space.
- Seal and cook on grill or grate over wood fire, medium-low to medium heat and cook about 20 minutes until done.

CABBAGE *Serve this with grilled sausages or bratwurst.*

3 cups shredded cabbage or cole slaw mix

1 cup chopped celery

1 onion, chopped

1 tablespoon vegetable oil

½ teaspoon salt

- Heat oil in skillet, add the rest, and cook covered for about 6-7 minutes.

Carrots

BASIC COOKED CARROTS

1—1 pound package baby carrots or 1 large carrot per person, peeled and sliced on the diagonal

2-3 tablespoons water

STEAMED

Place carrots on a double thickness of aluminum foil with enough extra foil to make a packet with a bit of air space.

Add water and seal.

Place on medium-low to medium heat and cook 20-25 minutes until done.

BOILED

Place in boiling water and cook about 6-8 minutes.

WITH PEACH GLAZE

1 recipe cooked carrots as above

1/3 cup peach preserves or jam

1 tablespoon butter

- Add to hot cooked carrots and let melt.

ORANGE AND CINNAMON FLAVORED

Prepare to steam carrots in aluminum foil pouch as above, but before sealing, stir together and add:

2/3 cup orange juice

½ teaspoon cornstarch

¼ teaspoon cinnamon

GINGERED APRICOT CARROTS

1 recipe cooked carrots as above

Stir into cooked carrots:

    2 teaspoons frozen orange juice concentrate (still frozen)

    1 tablespoon apricot preserves or jam

    several dashes ground ginger

CAULIFLOWER *Serve plain or with butter and cheese.*

1 head cauliflower or less, cut into flowerets, sliced into fork-sized pieces

½ -1 cup shredded Cheddar cheese (optional)

½ cup water

½ stick butter (optional)

- Place pieces on a double thickness of aluminum foil with enough extra foil to make a packet with a bit of air space.
- Add water and seal.
- Place on medium-low to medium heat and cook 20 minutes until done.
- Drain and serve or add butter and cheese, seal, and let melt.

Corn on the Cob *So many ways to savor this summertime icon!*

BOILED Plunge husked ears into boiling water and let boil 5 minutes.

GRILLED Husk and grill about 15 minutes, basting with butter and turning.

STEAMED Grill in husks or husk and wrap each ear in aluminum foil. If grilling in husk, soak ears in water 15 minutes or so before placing on grill for 15-20 minutes. Husks will blacken, but the corn will be delightfully moist.

ANOTHER IDEA: Husk ears and brush with butter before rolling each ear in aluminum foil. Can also sprinkle with dill weed or chili powder or a little grated Parmesan cheese after buttering.

Butters and Other Ideas for Corn

HOT CAJUN BUTTER
¼ cup softened butter
1 tablespoon commercial Cajun seasoning
2-3 drops liquid hot sauce

CHILI GARLIC BUTTER
¼ cup softened butter
1 teaspoon chili powder
½ teaspoon garlic salt

SOUTHWESTERN BUTTER

¼ cup softened butter

1-2 tablespoons chopped cilantro

2 teaspoons lime juice

¼ teaspoon cayenne

salt and pepper

LIME JUICE

Fresh lime wedges—1 per ear of corn

butter

salt

chili powder (optional)

- Squeeze lime over hot, cooked ear of corn.
- Slather with butter and sprinkle with salt and chili powder if you want.

OFF THE COB *If you have any cooked ears left over: Slice kernels off the cob and use in salsa, a breakfast omelette or frittata, add to a green salad, or freeze to enjoy the fresh taste of corn during the winter.*

Green Beans

Green beans can also be boiled, steamed, or grilled. Start with one pound fresh green beans, snap or snip off the stem end, leave whole or cut into pieces. You can find these bagged and ready to cook in the coolers in the salad area of the grocery.

BOIL Place in boiling water and cook about 7-8 minutes. Plunge into an ice bath.

GRILL Toss with oil and place on aluminum foil or grill topper. Grill, turning, about 6-8 minutes.

STEAM Make aluminum foil packet using double thickness foil, drizzle lightly with oil, and seal. Grill about 8-10 minutes.

GREEN BEANS AND CASHEWS

1 recipe cooked green beans
¼ cup cashew pieces
3 tablespoons butter

- Melt butter in skillet and sauté cashews about 5 minutes.
- Toss with cooked green beans.

ANOTHER IDEA: Add 2 tablespoons honey and cook and stir one minute before tossing with green beans.

GREEN BEANS ALMANDINE WITH LEMON

1 recipe cooked green beans

2 tablespoons sliced, toasted almonds or slivered almonds

2 tablespoons lemon juice

1 tablespoon butter

salt and pepper

- Combine all but green beans in small pan or aluminum foil pouch and heat until butter is melted.
- Pour over cooked green beans.

GREEN BEANS AND TOMATOES *The first time I made this was at the End of the Trail campground in the Boundary Water Canoe Wilderness Area in the far north of Minnesota, listening to loons call as we prepared our supper.*

1 recipe cooked green beans

1-2 tomatoes cut into wedges

¼ cup minced onion

2 tablespoons butter

1 tablespoon brown sugar

2 teaspoons prepared mustard

1 teaspoon salt

1 teaspoon horseradish

- Place veggies on a double thickness of aluminum foil with enough extra foil to make a packet with a bit of air space.
- Combine brown sugar, mustard, salt, and horseradish and top the vegetables.
- Dot with butter and seal.
- Place on medium-low to medium heat and cook 10 minutes, just until tomatoes are cooked and flavors have blended.

GREEN ONIONS ON THE GRILL

2 bunches green onions, roots removed

3 tablespoons oil, separated

1 tablespoon red wine vinegar

¼ teaspoon liquid hot sauce

¼ teaspoon salt

2 dashes pepper

- Make vinaigrette: Shake 2 tablespoons oil, vinegar, hot sauce, salt, and pepper in tightly covered container. Set aside.
- Toss green onions in 1 tablespoon of olive oil and place horizontally on medium hot, sprayed grill or grill topper.
- Cook, turning often with tongs about 3-4 minutes until softened and slightly charred. Be careful not to lose one to the grill!
- Drizzle with vinaigrette.

Mushrooms *Great on skewers or sautéed and served with beef.*

SAUTÉED OR IN FOIL WITH WINE

8 ounces fresh mushrooms, sliced

¼ cup white wine or blush or most anything but a red

¼ cup butter

¼ teaspoon seasoned salt

1/8 teaspoon garlic powder

- Cook all but wine in foil packet or in butter in skillet until mushrooms are tender, about 6 minutes.
- Add wine, leave packet open, and cook another 5-6 minutes to reduce liquid.

GARLICKY MUSHROOMS WITH GREEN ONIONS

8 ounce package fresh mushrooms, sliced

¼ cup butter

1 bunch green onions, sliced with tops

2 teaspoons Worcestershire sauce

¼ teaspoon salt

¼ teaspoon pepper

1-2 cloves garlic minced or ½ teaspoon if from a jar

- Melt butter in skillet and sauté green onions 2 minutes.
- Add mushrooms and the remaining ingredients.
- Cook, medium low until mushrooms are cooked through.

SPINACH, WILTED IN SKILLET *It will look like too much spinach when you add it to the pan, but it will reduce to about one-sixth its original size. Once wilted, it doesn't keep, so only make what you think will be eaten at the meal.*

This recipe is also wonderful using fresh leaf lettuce from the garden or farmers' market.

2—10 ounce bags baby spinach

3 tablespoons olive oil

2 tablespoons cider vinegar

1 tablespoon minced garlic or 3 teaspoons if from a jar

½ teaspoon red pepper flakes

salt

- Heat oil in skillet, sauté garlic 1 minute, and add red pepper flakes.
- Add vinegar and heat to rolling boil.
- Add spinach to skillet, tossing until wilted from the hot oil mixture.
- Sprinkle with salt and serve immediately.

SUMMER SQUASH *Mixes well with other vegetables in grilled dishes or salads. Pair with zucchini slices for color.*

3 yellow summer squash, sliced diagonally into ½ inch "planks" or split horizontally
2 tablespoons melted butter
2 dashes liquid hot sauce
grated Parmesan cheese

- Add hot sauce to melted butter and brush slices on one side only.
- Grill on medium hot grill, buttered side down, about 3-4 minutes.
- Turn, top with cheese and close grill or tent with aluminum foil if no way to cover the grill until cheese melts.

ANOTHER IDEA: Brush squash with commercial Italian dressing before placing on grill and again when turning.

Tomatoes on the Grill *Tomatoes can be cut in half or sliced in ½ inch slices.*

BASIC GRILLED TOMATOES

2 large slicing tomatoes
2 tablespoons olive oil
2 garlic cloves, minced, or 1 teaspoon if from a jar
salt and pepper

- Mix oil and garlic and brush on tomato halves or one side if sliced.
- Sprinkle with salt and pepper, place on medium hot grill, and cook 3-4 minutes if halved and 2 minutes per side if sliced, basting the second side when turned.

CREAMY PARMESAN TOPPED GRILLED TOMATOES *These look and taste like you slaved for hours!*

2 large slicing tomatoes, sliced in ½ inch slices

2 tablespoons mayonnaise or salad dressing blend

2 tablespoons sour cream or lite sour cream

1 tablespoon grated Parmesan cheese

1-2 teaspoons lemon juice

2-3 dashes garlic salt

- Combine mayo, sour cream, Parmesan, lemon juice, and garlic salt.
- Place tomato slices on medium hot grill and top each with some of the mayonnaise mixture.
- Grill, medium heat, until bubbly, about 5 minutes.

ITALIAN TOMATOES AU GRATIN IN FOIL

2 large slicing tomatoes, sliced in ½ inch slices

1/3 cup Italian-flavored bread crumbs

2 tablespoons grated Parmesan cheese

1 tablespoon butter

¼ teaspoon dried basil

- Place tomato slices on a double thickness of aluminum foil with enough extra foil to make a packet with a bit of air space.
- Combine bread crumbs, cheese, and basil and top the vegetables.
- Dot with butter and seal.
- Place on medium-low to medium heat and cook about 15-20 minutes, just until tomatoes are cooked and flavors have blended.

Zucchini *See "Summer Squash" above.*

LEMON GARLIC ZUCCHINI IN FOIL

3-4 medium zucchini, sliced on the diagonal into ½ inch planks

1-2 cloves garlic, minced, or ½ teaspoon if from a jar

2 tablespoons olive oil

2 tablespoons lemon juice

salt and pepper

- Assemble in foil packet and grill, medium, 20 minutes.

GRILLED ZUCCHINI

3-4 medium zucchini, sliced in half horizontally

1 bottle commercial Italian salad dressing

- Place zucchini on grill and brush with dressing.
- Grill, medium, about 10-12 minutes.

GRILLED VEGETABLE MEDLEY

1--8 ounce package sliced fresh mushrooms

1—8 ounce package baby carrots

5-6 new red potatoes, sliced in half

1 large yellow squash, sliced in ½ inch slices, diagonally?

1 medium to small zucchini, sliced in ½ inch slices, diagonally?

¼ cup olive oil or vegetable oil

½ packet dry onion soup mix

1 teaspoon crushed rosemary (optional)

- Toss everything in a large bowl or pan—or toss in two batches if there isn't enough room to combine it all at once.
- Make two grill packets of equal size and seal, leaving air space.
- Grill, covered grill, medium heat, 25-30 minutes until tender.

Sauces and Butters for Vegetables *Go from ordinary to "Wow!"*

CREAMY ONION

½ cup mayonnaise or salad dressing blend

1 tablespoon Dijon mustard

1 green onion and top, thinly sliced

HOT AND CREAMY

½ cup mayonnaise or salad dressing blend

½ teaspoon Worcestershire sauce

½ teaspoon prepared mustard

½ teaspoon liquid hot sauce

OH, SO GOOD! *This sauce is great with shrimp, wings, or grilled chicken breasts. Or spread on a wrap. Makes a lot, but multiple uses!*

1 ½ cups mayonnaise or salad dressing blend

¼ cup prepared horseradish

3 tablespoons lemon juice

2 tablespoons Worcestershire sauce

2 tablespoons minced onion

1 teaspoon salt

¼ teaspoon liquid hot sauce

1 clove garlic minced or ¼ teaspoon if from a jar

HERBED BUTTER WITH PARMESAN

1 stick butter, softened

¼ cup grated Parmesan cheese

3 tablespoons minced parsley

½ teaspoon Italian seasoning or dried oregano or basil

¼ teaspoon garlic salt

¼ teaspoon pepper

MUSTARD BUTTER

½ stick butter, softened

3 tablespoons finely chopped parsley

2 tablespoons grainy mustard

2 teaspoons prepared horseradish

1 teaspoon honey

LEMON BUTTER

½ stick butter, softened

2 green onions and tops, thinly sliced

1 teaspoon lemon juice

¼ teaspoon pepper

2-3 dashes cayenne

FRUIT and OTHER SWEET ENDINGS

Fresh Fruit Ideas

YOGURT FRUIT DIP

1 ¼ cup plain, low-fat yogurt

¼ cup orange marmalade

¼ teaspoon cinnamon

CREAMY HONEY FRUIT DIP

8 ounces sour cream or lite sour cream

¼ cup honey

¼ teaspoon cinnamon

CREAMY PEANUT BUTTER DIP

½ cup sour cream or lite sour cream

½ cup peanut butter

¼ cup orange juice concentrate, thawed but not diluted

2 tablespoons water

PEANUT BUTTER AND HONEY FRUIT DIP *Super with sliced apples and banana chunks on a toothpick!*

2/3 cup peanut butter
2/3 cup honey
¼ cup lemon juice

CARAMEL FRUIT DIP *Great with sliced apples!*

½ cup sour cream or lite sour cream
1 heaping tablespoon brown sugar
½ teaspoon cinnamon
¼ teaspoon ground ginger

YOGURT FRUIT SAUCE *Serve this on sliced oranges for breakfast.*

½ cup plain, low-fat yogurt
1 tablespoon honey
1/8 teaspoon cinnamon

Fruit on the Grill *Grilling brings out the sweetness in fruit, making it a great way to serve an easy, nutritious dessert.*

FRUIT KABOBS *Be sure to soak the skewers!*

1—8 ounce can pineapple chunks, drained and juice/syrup reserved

1 orange, peeled and sectioned

1 apple, cored, quartered, and then quarters cut in half

1 banana, cut into 1 inch chunks

3 tablespoons orange marmalade

¼ teaspoon ground ginger

- Make basting sauce: 2 tablespoons reserved pineapple juice blended with the marmalade and ginger and warmed in small pan or foil pouch to melt.
- Assemble kabobs and drizzle with sauce.
- Grill, turning and basting until heated through, 3-5 minutes.

GRILLED MIXED FRUIT WITH HONEY YOGURT SAUCE

8 ounces vanilla yogurt

2 tablespoons honey

peaches, cut in half and pit removed

pears, cut in half and core removed

bananas, peeled and cut into ½-3/4 inch chunks

fresh pineapple, peeled and cut into spears

- Make sauce: Combine yogurt and honey and chill.
- Place peaches and pears cut side down on grill or grill topper, close lid, and grill on medium heat 5-6 minutes and turn.
- Add banana slices and pineapple spears, close lid, and grill another 5-6 minutes.
- Serve with honey yogurt sauce.

GRILLED PEACHES

fresh peaches, cut in half and pit removed

½ cup apricot preserves or jam

2 tablespoons white wine vinegar

¼ teaspoon ground ginger

- Place peaches cut side down on grill or grill topper and grill on medium heat 4-5 minutes and turn.
- Baste with jam mixture and grill another 4 minutes.
- Serve with more jam mixture.

Pineapple *Fresh pineapple is wonderful on the grill! First cut off the bottom so you are working with a flat piece of fruit. Slice down the sides to remove all skin and "eyes" and don't worry about cutting off too much fruit as you do this. Biting into an "eye" is not pleasant, so cut them all off now. Cut pineapple into quarters and slice away the core. Now cut quarters into wedges or spears. You can leave the top on for eye appeal or cut off.*

GRILLED PINEAPPLE

pineapple spears

2 tablespoons melted butter

½ cup sour cream

2-3 tablespoons brown sugar

dash ginger

- Place pineapple on grill and brush with butter.
- Close lid and grill, medium, 3-4 minutes, turn, baste, and grill another 3-4 minutes.
- Combine brown sugar, ginger, and sour cream and serve each spear with a dollop on top.

RUM GLAZED GRILLED PINEAPPLE

pineapple spears

2 tablespoons rum

2 tablespoons honey

1 tablespoon lime juice

- Make glaze: Combine rum, honey, and lime juice.
- Place pineapple on grill and brush with glaze.
- Grill, medium, 3-4 minutes, turn, baste, and grill another 3-4 minutes.
- Baste first side again with glaze and serve.

Fruit in Foil

BAKED APPLES

one apple per person, cored and sliced, but not peeled

squirt of lemon juice per packet

2 tablespoons water per packet

TOPPINGS

orange marmalade

chopped pecans

raisins

cinnamon

- Have each diner assemble his own packet: Apple slices and any of the toppings desired, squirt of lemon juice, and the water.
- Seal securely and grill, medium, 20 minutes.

BANANA BITES *My grown kids and their friends had as much fun taste-testing these as the grandkids did!*

Start everyone off with ½ banana per person, peeled and cut into 3-4 pieces on a piece of aluminum foil big enough to make a pouch. Put each diner in charge of his own packet. Assemble individual packets, seal loosely, and grill, medium, about 4-5 minutes. Serve with a spoon.

#1: CHOCOLATE CHIPS AND MARSHMALLOWS

mini-marshmallows
dark chocolate chips or milk chocolate chips

#2: RUM SAUCE

¾ cup packed brown sugar
3 tablespoons butter
3 tablespoons rum

- Combine sugar, butter, and rum in small pan or pouch and heat to blend.
- Pour over banana pieces, seal pouch, and grill.

#3: PEANUT BUTTER AND HONEY

1 tablespoon peanut butter
drizzle with honey

#4: SPICE GLAZED

1 tablespoon butter
dash cinnamon
dash ginger

PEACHES WITH MARSHMALLOWS AND PECANS

½ fresh peach per person

1 tablespoon brown sugar per person

mini-marshmallows

pecan pieces

- Have each diner assemble his own pouch: Peach half, cut side up, topped with brown sugar, marshmallows, and pecans.
- Loosely close top so the marshmallow won't get stuck to the foil.
- Grill about 6-8 minutes, each diner in charge of his or her own packet.

PEACHES WITH RUM SAUCE

½ fresh peach per person

½ cup packed brown sugar

½ stick butter

1 tablespoon rum

crushed gingersnaps

- Mix butter, sugar, and rum with a fork.
- Have each diner assemble his own pouch: Peach half, cut side up, topped with a dollop of the butter mixture.
- Loosely close top and grill, low heat, about 10-15 minutes, each diner in charge of his packet.
- Top with crushed gingersnaps and serve.

PEARS

½ fresh pear per person, peeled and cut into 4 wedges

¼ cup orange juice

2 tablespoons brown sugar

2 tablespoons butter

1 tablespoon honey

½ teaspoon cinnamon

- Make syrup: Combine all but pear pieces in small pan or foil pouch and warm until combined.
- Have each diner assemble his own pouch: Pear pieces and then some of the syrup.
- Loosely close top and grill, medium low heat, 10 minutes, each diner in charge of his packet.
- Open packet and grill another 5 minutes.

FROZEN FRUIT

Individual servings: Thaw a package or two of frozen fruit such as mixed berries and top each serving with a dollop of sour cream and a spoonful of brown sugar.

Serve over angel food cake or pound cake: Purchase the cake and a package of frozen fruit such as sliced strawberries. Thaw fruit and stir in ¼ cup sugar and let sit for 10-15 minutes before spooning over cake.

Other Sweet Endings

S'MORES *I think these have been around forever!*

#1:TRADITIONAL
graham cracker

½ of chocolate candy bar

marshmallow, regular sized (The giant ones look cool, but the inside doesn't get gooey.)

- Break cracker in half so you have two equal-sized squares.
- Place chocolate bar half on one of the cracker squares.
- Cook marshmallow on a peeled stick or hot dog fork over the coals of a wood fire until marshmallow is puffy and golden----or aflame if you're not careful!
- Place marshmallow on chocolate square, using the remaining graham cracker square to help remove the marshmallow from the stick or hot dog fork.
- Top with graham cracker square.

#2: LAZY MAN'S WAY
- Make a foil packet with the graham cracker on the bottom.
- Top with chocolate bar or milk chocolate pieces and mini-marshmallows.
- Put second graham cracker square on top and loosely close packet.
- Grill, medium, about 4-5 minutes. You may need to eat it with a spoon.

GINGERSNAPS *I discovered these a couple summers ago, finding they make a nice, small, sweet ending for a summer dinner. Leftover spreads are good on bagels, too.*

1 box purchased gingersnaps

#1: CREAMY HONEY NUT SPREAD

1—8 ounce package cream cheese or Neufchatel (1/3 less fat)

¼ cup sour cream or lite sour cream

2 tablespoons honey

¼ cup chopped pecan pieces

#2: PINEAPPLE CREAM CHEESE

1—8 ounce package cream cheese or Neufchatel (1/3 less fat)

1—8 ounce can crushed pineapple, drained

#3: MASCARPONE *If you're not familiar with this, it is simply Italian cream cheese and can be found with other cheeses in the dairy case. It needs no embellishments--- just open the tub, put out a couple canapé knives, and sit back!*

#4: GRILLED BRIE *See "Grilled Brie" in Chapter 1.*

CPSIA information can be obtained at www.ICGtesting.com
Printed in the USA
BVOW01s2204180614

356760BV00004B/7/P